DEPARTMENT OF THE TREASURY TECHNICAL EXPLANATION OF THE CONVENTION BETWEEN THE GOVERNMENT OF THE UNITED STATES OF AMERICA AND THE GOVERNMENT OF THE REPUBLIC OF CHILE FOR THE AVOIDANCE OF DOUBLE TAXATION AND THE PREVENTION OF FISCAL EVASION WITH RESPECT TO TAXES ON INCOME AND CAPITAL

DEPARTMENT OF THE TREASURY TECHNICAL EXPLANATION OF THE CONVENTION BETWEEN THE GOVERNMENT OF THE UNITED STATES OF AMERICA AND THE GOVERNMENT OF THE REPUBLIC OF CHILE FOR THE AVOIDANCE OF DOUBLE TAXATION AND THE PREVENTION OF FISCAL EVASION WITH RESPECT TO TAXES ON INCOME AND CAPITAL

This is a Technical Explanation of the Convention between the Government of the United States and the Government of the Republic of Chile for the Avoidance of Double Taxation and the Prevention of Fiscal Evasion with Respect to Taxes on Income and Capital, signed on February 4, 2010 (the "Convention") as well as an amending Protocol signed the same day (the "Protocol").

Negotiations on the Convention took into account the U.S. Treasury Department's current tax treaty policy and the Treasury Department's Model Income Tax Convention, published on November 15, 2006 (the "U.S. Model"). Negotiations also took into account the Model Tax Convention on Income and on Capital, published by the Organisation for Economic Cooperation and Development (the "OECD Model"), and recent tax treaties concluded by both countries.

On the date of signing of the Convention and the Protocol, the United States and Chile also exchanged diplomatic Notes (the "2010 Exchange of Notes") relating to various provisions of the Convention and the Protocol. The United States and Chile also exchanged diplomatic Notes on February 25, 2011 (the "2011 Exchange of Notes") and on February 10 and 21, 2012 (the "2012 Exchange of Notes"). The 2010, 2011, and 2012 Exchanges of Notes constitute an integral part of the overall agreement between the United States and Chile.

The Technical Explanation is an official guide to the Convention, Protocol, and Exchanges of Notes. It reflects the policies behind particular Convention provisions, as well as understandings reached during the negotiations with respect to the application and interpretation of the Convention, Protocol, and Exchanges of Notes. References in the Technical Explanation to "he" or "his" should be read to mean "he or she" or "his and her." References to the "Code" are to the Internal Revenue Code of 1986, as amended.

ARTICLE 1 (GENERAL SCOPE)

Article 1 provides that the Convention applies only to residents of the United States or Chile except where the terms of the Convention provide otherwise. Under Article 4 (Residence) a person is generally treated as a resident of a Contracting State if that person is, under the laws of that State, liable to tax therein by reason of his domicile, residence, citizenship, place of management, place of incorporation, or any other criterion of a similar nature. However, if a person is considered a resident of both Contracting States, Article 4 provides rules for determining a State of residence (or no Contracting State of residence). This determination governs for all purposes of the Convention.

Certain provisions are applicable to persons who may not be residents of either Contracting State. For example, paragraph 1 of Article 25 (Non-Discrimination) applies to nationals of the Contracting States. In addition, under Article 27 (Exchange of Information), information may be exchanged with respect to residents of third states.

Paragraph 2 of the Protocol states the generally accepted relationship both between the Convention and domestic law and between the Convention and other agreements to which both of the Contracting States are parties. That is, no provision in the Convention may restrict any exclusion, exemption, deduction, credit or other allowance or benefit accorded by the tax laws of the Contracting States, or by any other agreement between the Contracting States. The relationship between the non-discrimination provisions of the Convention and the General Agreement on Trade in Services (the "GATS") is addressed in paragraph 3 of the Protocol.

Under paragraph 2 of the Protocol, for example, if a deduction would be allowed under the Code in computing the U.S. taxable income of a resident of Chile, the deduction also is allowed to that person in computing taxable income under the Convention. Paragraph 2 also means that the Convention may not increase the tax burden on a resident of a Contracting State beyond the burden determined under domestic law. Thus, a right to tax permitted by the Convention cannot be exercised unless that right also exists under domestic law.

It follows that, under the principle of paragraph 2 of the Protocol, a taxpayer's U.S. tax liability need not be determined under the Convention if the Code would produce a more favorable result. A taxpayer may not, however, choose among the provisions of the Code and the Convention in an inconsistent manner in order to minimize tax. Thus, a taxpayer may use the Convention to reduce its taxable income, but may not combine both treaty and Code rules in a way that would be inconsistent with the intent of either set of rules. For example, assume that a resident of Chile has three separate businesses in the United States. One is a profitable permanent establishment and the other two are trades or businesses that would earn taxable income under the Code but that do not meet the permanent establishment threshold tests of the Convention. One is profitable and the other incurs a loss. Under the Convention, the income of the permanent establishment is taxable in the United States, and both the profit and loss of the other two businesses are ignored. Under the Code, all three would be subject to tax, but the loss would offset the profits of the two profitable ventures. The taxpayer may not invoke the Convention to exclude the profits of the profitable trade or business and invoke the Code to claim the loss of the loss trade or business against the profit of the permanent establishment. *See* Rev. Rul. 84-17, 1984-1 C.B. 308. If, however, the taxpayer invokes the Code for the taxation of all three ventures, he would not be precluded from invoking the Convention with respect, for example, to any dividend income he may receive from the United States that is not effectively connected with any of his business activities in the United States.

Similarly, except as provided in paragraph 3, nothing in the Convention can be used to deny any benefit granted by any other agreement between the United States and Chile. For example, if certain benefits are provided for military personnel or military contractors under a Status of Forces Agreement between the United States and Chile, those benefits or protections will be available to residents of the Contracting States regardless of any provisions to the contrary (or silence) in the Convention.

Paragraph 3 of the Protocol relates to non-discrimination obligations of the Contracting States under the GATS. The provisions of paragraph 3 are an exception to the rule provided in paragraph 2 of the Protocol under which the Convention shall not restrict in any manner any benefit now or hereafter accorded by any other agreement between the Contracting States.

Subparagraph 3(a) of the Protocol provides that, unless the competent authorities determine that a taxation measure is not within the scope of the Convention, the national treatment obligations of the GATS shall not apply with respect to that measure. Further, any question arising as to the interpretation or application of the Convention, including in particular whether a measure is within the scope of the Convention, shall be considered only by the competent authorities of the Contracting States, and the procedures under the Convention exclusively shall apply to the dispute. Thus, paragraph 3 of Article XXII (Consultation) of the GATS may not be used to bring a dispute before the World Trade Organization unless the competent authorities of both Contracting States have determined that the relevant taxation measure is not within the scope of Article 25 (Non-Discrimination) of the Convention.

The term "measure" for these purposes is defined broadly in paragraph 3 of the Protocol. It would include a law, regulation, rule, procedure, decision, administrative action or guidance, or any other similar provision or action.

Paragraph 4 of the Protocol contains the traditional saving clause found in all U.S. income tax treaties. The Contracting States reserve their rights, except as provided otherwise in paragraph 4 of the Protocol, to tax their residents and citizens as provided under their domestic laws, notwithstanding any provisions of the Convention to the contrary. For example, if a resident of Chile performs professional services in the United States and the income from the services is not attributable to a permanent establishment in the United States, Article 7 (Business Profits) would by its terms prevent the United States from taxing the income. If, however, the resident of Chile is also a citizen of the United States, the saving clause permits the United States to include the remuncration in the worldwide income of the citizen and subject it to tax under the normal Code rules (*i.e.*, without regard to Code section 894(a)). Paragraph 4 of the Protocol also preserves the benefits of special foreign tax credit rules applicable to the U.S. taxation of certain U.S. income of its citizens resident in Chile. *See* paragraph 5 of Article 23 (Relief from Double Taxation).

For purposes of the saving clause, "residence" is determined under Article 4 (Residence). Thus, an individual who is a resident of the United States under the Code (but not a U.S. citizen) but who is determined to be a resident of the other Contracting State under the tie-breaker rules of Article 4 would be subject to U.S. tax only to the extent permitted by the Convention. The United States would not be permitted to apply its domestic law to that person to the extent that its law is inconsistent with the Convention.

However, the person would still be treated as a U.S. resident for U.S. tax purposes other than determining the individual's U.S. tax liability. For example, in determining under Code section 957 whether a foreign corporation is a controlled foreign corporation, shares in that corporation held by the individual would be considered to be held by a U.S. resident. As a result, other U.S. citizens or residents might be deemed to be United States shareholders of a controlled foreign corporation subject to current inclusion of subpart F income recognized by the corporation. *See* Treas. Reg. § 301.7701(b)-7(a)(3).

Under paragraph 4 of the Protocol, each Contracting State also reserves its right to tax former citizens and former long-term residents for a period of ten years following the loss of such status. Thus, paragraph 4 allows the United States to tax former U.S. citizens and former U.S. long-term residents in accordance with Code section 877. Section 877 generally applies to a former citizen or long-term resident of the United States who relinquishes citizenship or terminates long-term residency before June 17, 2008, if he fails to certify that he has complied with U.S. tax laws during the 5 preceding years, or if either of the following criteria exceed established thresholds: (a) the average annual net income tax of such individual for the period of 5 taxable years ending before the date of the loss of status; or (b) the net worth of such individual as of the date of the loss of status.

The United States defines "long-term resident" as an individual (other than a U.S. citizen) who is a lawful permanent resident of the United States in at least 8 of the prior 15 taxable years. An individual is not treated as a lawful permanent resident for any taxable year in which the individual is treated as a resident of Chile under this Convention, or as a resident of any country other than the United States under the provisions of any other U.S. tax treaty, and the individual does not waive the benefits of the relevant tax treaty.

Subparagraphs 4(a) and 4(b) of the Protocol set forth certain exceptions to the saving clause. The referenced provisions are intended to preserve benefits for citizens and residents of the Contracting States even if such benefits do not exist under domestic law.

Subparagraph 4(a) of the Protocol lists certain provisions of the Convention that are applicable to all citizens and residents of a Contracting State, despite the general saving clause rule of paragraph 4:

(1) Paragraph 2 of Article 9 (Associated Enterprises) grants the right to a correlative adjustment with respect to income tax due on profits reallocated under Article 9.

(2) Paragraphs 1 (b), 3, 4, and 6 of Article 18 (Pensions, Social Security, Alimony and Child Support) provide exemptions from source or residence State taxation for certain pension distributions, social security payments, investment income of pension funds located in the other Contracting State, alimony, and child support.

(3) Article 23 (Relief from Double Taxation) confers to citizens and residents of one Contracting State the benefit of a credit for income taxes paid to the other or an exemption for income earned in the other State.

(4) Article 25 (Non-Discrimination) protects residents and nationals of one Contracting State against the adoption of certain discriminatory taxation practices in the other Contracting State.

(5) Article 26 (Mutual Agreement Procedure) confers certain benefits on citizens and residents of the Contracting States in order to reach and implement solutions to disputes between the two Contracting States. For example, the competent authorities are permitted to use a definition of a term that differs from an internal law definition. The statute of limitations may be waived for refunds, so that the benefits of an agreement may be implemented.

Subparagraph 4(b) of the Protocol provides a different set of exceptions to the saving clause. The benefits referred to are all intended to be granted to temporary residents of a Contracting State (for example, in the case of the United States, holders of non-immigrant visas), but not to citizens or to persons who have acquired permanent residence in that State. If beneficiaries of these provisions travel from one of the Contracting States to the other, and remain in the other long enough to become residents under its internal law, but do not acquire permanent residence status (*i.e.*, in the U.S. context, they do not become "green card" holders) and are not citizens of that State, the host State will continue to grant these benefits even if they conflict with the statutory rules. The benefits preserved by this paragraph are: the host country exemptions for certain pension distributions and the beneficial tax treatment of pension fund contributions under paragraphs 2 and 5 of Article 18 (Pensions, Social Security, Alimony and Child Support); government service salaries and pensions under Article 19 (Government Service); certain income of visiting students, apprentices, and trainees under Article 20 (Students and Trainees); and the income of diplomatic agents and consular officers under Article 28 (Members of Diplomatic Missions and Consular Posts).

Paragraph 1 of the Protocol addresses special issues presented by fiscally transparent entities such as partnerships and certain estates and trusts. Because countries may take different views as to when an entity is fiscally transparent, the risks of both double taxation and double non-taxation are relatively high. The intention of paragraph 1 of the Protocol is to eliminate a number of technical problems that arguably would have prevented investors using such entities from claiming treaty benefits, even though such investors would be subject to tax on the income derived through such entities. The provision also prevents the use of such entities to claim treaty benefits in circumstances where the person investing through such an entity is not subject to tax on the income in its State of residence. The provision, and the corresponding requirements of other Articles of the Convention, should be interpreted with those two goals in mind.

In general, this paragraph applies to any resident of a Contracting State who is entitled to income derived through an entity that is treated as fiscally transparent under the laws of either Contracting State. Treas. Reg. § 1.894-1(d)(3)(iii) provides that an entity will be fiscally transparent under the laws of an interest holder's jurisdiction with respect to an item of income to the extent that the laws of that jurisdiction require the interest holder resident in that jurisdiction to separately take into account on a current basis the interest holder's respective share of the item of income paid to the entity, whether or not distributed to the interest holder, and the character and source of the item in the hands of the interest holder are determined as if such item were realized directly by the interest holder. Entities falling under this description in the United States include partnerships, corporations that have made a valid election to be taxed under Subchapter S of Chapter 1 of the Code ("S" corporations), common investment trusts under section 584, simple trusts, and grantor trusts. This paragraph also applies to other entities that are treated as partnerships or as disregarded entities for U.S. tax purposes, such as U.S. limited liability companies ("LLCs").

Under paragraph 1 of the Protocol, an item of income, profit or gain derived by such a fiscally transparent entity will be considered to be derived by a resident of a Contracting State if a resident is treated under the taxation laws of that State as deriving the item of income. For example, if a company that is a resident of Chile pays interest to an entity that is treated as fiscally transparent for U.S. tax purposes, the interest will be considered derived by a resident of the United States only to the extent that the taxation laws of the United States treat one or more U.S. residents (whose status as U.S. residents is determined, for this purpose, under U.S. tax law) as deriving the interest for U.S. tax purposes. In the case of a partnership, the persons who are, under U.S. tax laws, treated as partners of the entity would normally be the persons whom the U.S. tax laws would treat as deriving the interest income through the partnership. Also, it follows that persons whom the United States treats as partners but who are not U.S. residents for U.S. tax purposes may not claim a benefit for the interest paid to the entity, because they are not residents of the United States for purposes of claiming this benefit. If, however, the country in which they are treated as resident for tax purposes, as determined under the laws of that country, has an income tax convention with Chile, they may be entitled to claim a benefit under that convention. In contrast, if, for example, an entity is organized under U.S. laws and is classified as a corporation for U.S. tax purposes, interest paid by a company that is a resident of Chile to the U.S. entity will be considered derived by a resident of the United States since the U.S. corporation is treated under U.S. taxation laws as a resident of the United States and as deriving the income.

The same result would be reached even if the tax laws of Chile would treat the entity differently (*e.g.*, if the entity were not treated as fiscally transparent in the source State in the first example above where the entity is treated as a partnership for U.S. tax purposes). The results follow regardless of whether the entity is disregarded as a separate entity under the laws of one jurisdiction but not the other, such as a single-owner entity that is viewed as a branch for U.S. tax purposes and as a corporation for tax purposes under the laws of Chile. Similarly, the characterization of the entity in a third country is also irrelevant, even if the entity is organized in that third country. The outcome would be identical regardless of where the entity is organized (*i.e.*, in the United States, in Chile, or as noted above, in a third country), subject to the saving clause of paragraph 4.

For example, income from U.S. sources received by an entity organized under the laws of the United States, which is treated for tax purposes under the laws of Chile as a corporation and is owned by a shareholder who is a resident of Chile for its tax purposes, is not considered derived by the shareholder of that corporation even if, under the tax laws of the United States, the entity is treated as fiscally transparent. Rather, for purposes of the treaty, the income is treated as derived by the U.S. entity.

These principles also apply to trusts to the extent that they are fiscally transparent in either Contracting State. For example, if X, a resident of Chile, creates a revocable trust in the United States and names persons resident in a third country as the beneficiaries of the trust, the trust's income would be regarded as being derived by a resident of Chile only to the extent that the laws of Chile treat X as deriving the income for its tax purposes, perhaps through application of rules similar to the U.S. "grantor trust" rules.

Paragraph 1 of the Protocol is not an exception to the saving clause of paragraph 4 of the Protocol. Accordingly, paragraph 1 does not prevent a Contracting State from taxing an entity that is treated as a resident of that State under its tax law. For example, if a U.S. LLC with members who are residents of Chile elects to be taxed as a corporation for U.S. tax purposes, the United States will tax that LLC on its worldwide income on a net basis, without regard to whether Chile views the LLC as fiscally transparent.

ARTICLE 2 (TAXES COVERED)

This Article specifies the U.S. taxes and the taxes of Chile to which the Convention applies. With two exceptions, the taxes specified in Article 2 are the covered taxes for all purposes of the Convention. A broader coverage applies, however, for purposes of Articles 25 (Non-Discrimination) and 27 (Exchange of Information). Article 25 applies with respect to taxes of every kind and description imposed by a Contracting State or a political subdivision or local authority thereof, except that in the case of taxes not covered by the Convention, Article 25 does not apply to any tax laws of a Contracting State that are in force on the date of signature of the Convention. Article 27 applies with respect to all taxes imposed at the national level.

Paragraph 1

Paragraph 1 identifies the categories of taxes to which the Convention applies. Paragraph 1 is based on the U.S. and OECD Models and defines the scope of application of the Convention. The Convention applies to taxes on income and on capital, including gains, imposed on behalf of a Contracting State, irrespective of the manner in which they are levied. Except with respect to Article 25 (Non-Discrimination), state and local taxes are not covered by the Convention.

Paragraph 2

Paragraph 2 also is based on the U.S. and OECD Models and provides a definition of taxes on income and on capital. The Convention covers taxes on total income, on total capital, or on any part of income or of capital, and includes taxes on gains derived from the alienation of property as well as taxes on capital appreciation. The Convention does not apply, however, to social security or unemployment taxes, or any other charges where there is a direct connection between the levy and individual benefits. Nor does it apply to property taxes, except with respect to Article 25 (Non-Discrimination).

Paragraph 3

Paragraph 3 lists the taxes in force at the time of signature of the Convention to which the Convention applies. Subparagraph 3(a) provides that the existing U.S. taxes subject to the rules of the Convention are the Federal income taxes imposed by the Code, together with the Federal excise taxes imposed on insurance premiums paid to foreign insurers (Code sections 4371 through 4374) and with respect to private foundations (Code sections 4940 through 4948). Social security and unemployment taxes (Code sections 1401, 3101, 3111 and 3301) are specifically excluded from coverage. Subparagraph 3(b) provides that the existing covered taxes of Chile are the taxes imposed under the Income Tax Act (*Ley sobre Impuesto a la Renta*).

Paragraph 4

Under paragraph 4, the Convention will apply to any taxes that are identical, or substantially similar, to those enumerated in paragraph 3, and to taxes on capital, which are imposed in addition to, or in place of, the existing taxes after February 4, 2010, the date of signature of the Convention. The paragraph also provides that the competent authorities of the Contracting States will notify each other of any significant changes to their tax laws.

ARTICLE 3 (GENERAL DEFINITIONS)

Article 3 provides general definitions and rules of interpretation applicable throughout the Convention. Certain other terms are defined in other articles of the Convention. For example, the term "resident of a Contracting State" is defined in Article 4 (Residence). The term "permanent establishment" is defined in Article 5 (Permanent Establishment). These definitions apply for all purposes of the Convention. Other terms, such as "dividends," "interest," and "royalties" are defined in specific articles for purposes of those articles.

Paragraph 1

Paragraph 1 defines a number of basic terms used in the Convention. The introduction to paragraph 1 makes clear that these definitions apply for all purposes of the Convention, unless the context requires otherwise. This latter condition allows flexibility in the interpretation of the Convention in order to avoid results not intended by the Convention's negotiators.

The geographical scope of the Convention with respect to the United States is set out in subparagraphs 1(a) and 1(c). It encompasses the United States of America, including the states and the District of Columbia. The term does not include Puerto Rico, the Virgin Islands, Guam or any other U.S. possession. For certain purposes, the term "United States" includes the territorial sea of the United States, as well as the sea bed and subsoil of undersea areas adjacent to the territorial sea of the United States to the extent that the United States exercises sovereignty in accordance with international law for the purpose of natural resource exploration and exploitation of such areas. This extension of the definition applies, however, only if the person, property or activity to which the Convention is being applied is connected with such natural resource exploration or exploitation. Thus, it would not include any activity involving the sea floor of an area over which the United States exercised sovereignty for natural resource purposes if that activity was unrelated to the exploration and exploitation of natural resources. This result is consistent with the result that would be obtained under Section 638, which treats the continental shelf as part of the United States for purposes of natural resource exploration and exploitation.

The geographical scope of the Convention with respect to Chile is set out in subparagraphs 1(b) and 1(c). The term "Chile" means the Republic of Chile and includes the territorial sea thereof as well as the sea bed and subsoil of the submarine areas adjacent to the territorial sea over which Chile exercises sovereign rights in accordance with international law.

Subparagraph 1(d) defines the term "person" to include an individual, a company and any other body of persons. Paragraph 1 of the 2010 Exchange of Notes provides that the term "person" includes an estate, trust or partnership. The definition is significant for a variety of reasons. For example, under Article 4 (Residence), only a "person" can be a "resident" and therefore eligible for most benefits under the Convention. Also, all "persons" are eligible to claim relief under Article 26 (Mutual Agreement Procedure).

The term "company" is defined in subparagraph 1(e) as a body corporate or an entity treated as a body corporate for tax purposes in the state where it is organized. The definition refers to the law of the state in which an entity is organized in order to ensure that an entity that is treated as fiscally transparent in its country of residence will not get inappropriate benefits, such as the reduced withholding rate provided by subparagraph 2(a) of Article 10 (Dividends). It also ensures that the Limitation on Benefits provisions of Article 24 will be applied at the appropriate level.

The terms "enterprise of a Contracting State" and "enterprise of the other Contracting State" are defined in subparagraph (f) respectively as an enterprise carried on by a resident of a Contracting State and an enterprise carried on by a resident of the other Contracting State. An enterprise of a Contracting State need not be carried on in that State. It may be carried on in the other Contracting State or a third state (*e.g.*, a U.S. corporation doing all of its business in the other Contracting State would still be a U.S. enterprise).

Paragraph 2 of the 2010 Exchange of Notes provides that the terms defined in subparagraph 1(f) of Article 3 of the Convention include an enterprise conducted through an entity (such as a partnership) that is treated as fiscally transparent in the Contracting State where the entity's owner is resident. The definition makes this point explicitly to ensure that the purpose of the Convention is not thwarted by an overly technical application of the term "enterprise of a Contracting State" to activities carried on through partnerships and similar entities. In accordance with Article 4 (Resident), an entity that is fiscally transparent in the Contracting State in which it is organized is not considered to be a resident of that Contracting State (although income derived through such an entity may be treated as the income of a resident of a Contracting State to the extent that it is taxed in the hands of resident partners or other resident owners). The definition makes clear that an enterprise conducted by such an entity will be treated as carried on by a resident of a Contracting State to the extent its partners or other owners are residents. This approach is consistent with Code section 875, which attributes a trade or business conducted by a partnership to its partners and a trade or business conducted by an estate or trust to its beneficiaries.

Subparagraph 1(g) defines the term "international traffic." The term means any transport by a ship or aircraft except when such transport is solely between places within a Contracting State. This definition is applicable principally in the context of Article 8 (International Transport). The definition combines with paragraph 2 of Article 8 to exempt from tax by the source State profits from the rental of ships of or aircraft on a full (time or voyage) basis and profits from the rental on a bareboat basis of ships or aircraft if the rental income is incidental to profits from the operation of ships or aircraft in international traffic.

The exclusion from international traffic of transport solely between places within a Contracting State means, for example, that carriage of goods or passengers solely between New York and Chicago would not be treated as international traffic, whether carried by a U.S. or a foreign carrier. The substantive taxing rules of the Convention relating to the taxation of income from transport, principally Article 8 (International Transport), therefore, would not apply to income from such carriage. Thus, if the carrier engaged in internal U.S. traffic were a resident of Chile (assuming that were possible under U.S. law), the United States would not be required to exempt the income from that transport under Article 8. The income would, however, be treated as business profits under Article 7 (Business Profits), and therefore would be taxable in the United States only if attributable to a U.S. permanent establishment of the foreign carrier, and then only on a net basis. The gross basis U.S. tax imposed by section 887 would never apply under the circumstances described. If, however, goods or passengers were carried by a carrier resident in Chile from a non-U.S. port to, for example, New York, and some of the goods or passengers continued on to Chicago, the entire transport would be international traffic. This would be true if the international carrier transferred the goods at the U.S. port of entry from a ship to a land vehicle, from a ship to a lighter, or even if the overland portion of the trip in the United States was handled by an independent carrier under contract with the original international carrier, so long as both parts of the trip were reflected in original bills of lading. For this reason, the Convention, following the U.S. Model, refers, in the definition of "international traffic," to "such transport" being solely between places in the other Contracting State, while the OECD Model refers to the ship or aircraft being operated solely between such places. The formulation in the Convention is intended to make clear that, as in the above example, even if the goods are carried on a different aircraft for the internal portion of the international voyage than is used for the overseas portion of the trip, the definition applies to that internal portion as well as the external portion.

Finally, a "cruise to nowhere," *i.e.*, a cruise beginning and ending in a port in the same Contracting State with no stops in a foreign port, would not constitute international traffic.

Subparagraph 1(h) designates the "competent authorities" for the other Contracting State and the United States. The U.S. competent authority is the Secretary of the Treasury or his delegate. The Secretary of the Treasury has delegated the competent authority function to the

Commissioner of Internal Revenue, who in turn has delegated the authority to the Deputy Commissioner (International) LB&I of the Internal Revenue Service. With respect to interpretative issues, the Deputy Commissioner (International) LB&I acts with the concurrence of the Associate Chief Counsel (International) of the Internal Revenue Service. In the case of Chile, the competent authority is the Minister of Finance or his authorized representative.

The term "national," as it relates to the United States and to Chile, is defined in subparagraph 1(i). This term is relevant for purposes of Articles 4 (Residence), 19 (Government Service) and 25 (Non-Discrimination). A national of one of the Contracting States is (1) an individual who is a citizen or national of that State, and (2) any legal person, partnership or association deriving its status as such from the laws in force in the State where it is established.

Subparagraph 1(j) defines the term "pension fund." The term means any person that is established in a Contracting State and that satisfies two criteria. First, as provided in clause 1(j)(i), the person must be generally exempt from income taxation in the Contracting State in which it is established. Second, as provided in clause 1(j)(ii), the person must be operated principally either to administer or provide pension or retirement benefits, or to earn income only for the benefit of one or more persons established in the same Contracting State that are generally exempt from income taxation in that Contracting State and are operated principally to administer or provide pension or retirement benefits.

The definition recognizes that pension funds sometimes administer or provide benefits other than pension or retirement benefits, such as death benefits. However, in order for the fund to be considered a pension fund for purposes of the Convention, the provision of any other such benefits must be merely incidental to the fund's principal activity of administering or providing pension or retirement benefits. The definition also ensures that if a fund is a collective fund that earns income for the benefit of other funds, then each fund that participates in the collective fund must be a resident of the same Contracting State as the collective fund and must be entitled to benefits under the Convention in its own right.

In the case of the United States, the term "pension fund" includes the following: a trust providing pension or retirement benefits under a Code section 401(a) qualified pension plan (which includes a section 401(k) plan); a profit sharing or stock bonus plan; a Code section 403(a) qualified annuity plan; a Code section 403(b) plan; a trust that is an individual retirement account under Code section 408; a Roth individual retirement account under Code section 408A or a simple retirement account under Code section 408(p); a trust providing pension or retirement benefits under a simplified employee pension plan under Code section 408(k); a trust described in section 457(g) providing pension or retirement benefits under a Code section 457(b) plan; and the Thrift Savings Fund (section 7701(j)). A group trust described in Rev. Rul. 81-100, as amended by Rev. Rul. 2004-67 and Rev. Rul. 2011-1, qualifies as a pension fund only if each participant is a pension fund that is itself entitled to benefits under the Convention as a resident of the United States.

Paragraph 2

Terms that are not defined in the Convention are dealt with in paragraph 2. Paragraph 2 provides that in the application of the Convention, any term used but not defined in the Convention will have the meaning that it has under the law of the Contracting State whose tax is being applied, unless the context requires otherwise. If the term is defined under both the tax and non-tax laws of a Contracting State, the definition in the tax law will take precedence over the definition in the non-tax laws. Finally, there also may be cases where the tax laws of a State contain multiple definitions of the same term. In such a case, the definition used for purposes of the particular provision at issue, if any, should be used.

If the meaning of a term cannot be readily determined under the law of a Contracting State, or if there is a conflict in meaning under the laws of the two States that creates difficulties in the application of the Convention, the competent authorities, as indicated in paragraph 5 of the Protocol, may establish, pursuant to the provisions of Article 26 (Mutual Agreement Procedure), a common meaning in order to prevent double taxation or to further any other purpose of the Convention. This common meaning need not conform to the meaning of the term under the laws of either Contracting State.

The reference in paragraph 2 to the domestic law of a Contracting State means the law in effect at the time the treaty is being applied, not the law in effect at the time the treaty was signed. The use of ambulatory definitions, however, may lead to results that are at variance with the intentions of the negotiators and of the Contracting States when the treaty was negotiated and ratified. The inclusion in both paragraphs 1 and 2 of an exception to the generally applicable definitions where the "context otherwise requires" is intended to address this circumstance. Where reflecting the intent of the Contracting States requires the use of a definition that is different from a definition under paragraph 1 or the law of the Contracting State applying the Convention, that definition will apply. Thus, flexibility in defining terms is necessary and permitted.

ARTICLE 4 (RESIDENCE)

This Article sets forth rules for determining whether a person is a resident of a Contracting State for purposes of the Convention. As a general matter only residents of the Contracting States may claim the benefits of the Convention. The treaty definition of residence is to be used only for purposes of the Convention. The fact that a person is determined to be a resident of a Contracting State under Article 4 does not automatically entitle that person to the benefits of the Convention. In addition to being a resident, a person also must qualify for benefits under Article 24 (Limitation on Benefits) in order to receive benefits conferred on residents of a Contracting State.

The determination of residence for treaty purposes looks first to a person's liability to tax as a resident under the respective taxation laws of the Contracting States. As a general matter, a person who is liable to tax as a resident under the domestic laws of one Contracting State and not of the other is a resident of the State in which he is liable to tax as resident under domestic law. If, however, a person is liable to tax as a resident under the domestic laws of both Contracting

States, the Article uses tie-breaker rules to assign a single State of residence (or no State of residence) to such a person for purposes of the Convention.

Paragraph 1

The term "resident of a Contracting State" is defined in paragraph 1. In general, this definition incorporates the definitions of residence in U.S. law and that of Chile by referring to a resident as a person who, under the laws of a Contracting State, is liable to tax therein by reason of his domicile, residence, citizenship, place of management, place of incorporation or any other similar criterion. Thus, residents of the United States include aliens who are considered U.S. residents under Code section 7701(b). Paragraph 1 also specifically includes the two Contracting States, and political subdivisions and local authorities of the two States and any agency or instrumentality of the States, as residents for purposes of the Convention.

The fact that a particular entity does not pay tax in practice will not necessarily mean that the entity is not a resident. An entity that is not fiscally transparent in its Contracting State of residence for purposes of paragraph 1 of the Protocol, and is not unconditionally exempt from tax, will generally be treated as a resident for purposes of the Convention. This is generally true even for an entity that, in practice, is not required to pay tax if it meets certain requirements with respect to its activities, types of income, or distribution practices. For example, a U.S. Regulated Investment Company (RIC) and a U.S. Real Estate Investment Trust (REIT) are residents of the United States for purposes of the treaty. These entities are taxable to the extent that they do not currently distribute their profits, and therefore may be regarded as "liable to tax," even though these entities do not generally have taxable income in practice. They also must satisfy a number of requirements under the Code in order to be entitled to special tax treatment.

Under paragraph 1 of Article 4, a person who is liable to tax in a Contracting State only in respect of income from sources within that State or capital situated therein will not be treated as a resident of that Contracting State for purposes of the Convention. Thus, a consular official of Chile who is posted in the United States, who may be subject to U.S. tax on U.S. source investment income, but is not taxable in the United States on non-U.S. source income (*see* Code section 7701(b)(5)(B)), would not be considered a resident of the United States for purposes of the Convention. Under paragraph 3 of the 2010 Exchange of Notes, a person who is liable to tax in a Contracting State only on profits attributable to a permanent establishment in that State will also not be treated as a resident of that State for purposes of the Convention. Thus, an enterprise of Chile with a permanent establishment in the United States is not, by virtue of that permanent establishment, a resident of the United States. The enterprise generally is subject to U.S. tax only with respect to its income that is attributable to the U.S. permanent establishment, not with respect to its worldwide income, as it would be if it were a U.S. resident.

Paragraph 6 of the Protocol provides that entities such as pension funds as defined in Article 3 (General Definitions) and legal persons organized under the laws of a Contracting State and established exclusively for religious, charitable, scientific, artistic, cultural, or educational purposes are residents of the Contracting State in which they are established or organized. Such persons are liable to tax, notwithstanding that all or part of their income or gains may be exempt from tax under the domestic laws of that State. Thus, a section 501(c) organization organized in the United States (such as a U.S. charity) that is generally exempt from tax under U.S. law is nevertheless a resident of the United States for all purposes of the Convention.

Paragraph 7 of the Protocol provides that Chile shall treat a U.S. citizen or an alien lawfully admitted for permanent residence (a "green card holder") as a resident of the United States only if such individual has a substantial presence, permanent home, or habitual abode in the United States and if that individual is not a resident of a State other than Chile for purposes of a double taxation convention between that State and Chile.

Paragraph 2

If, under the domestic law of both Contracting States, and, thus, under paragraph 1, an individual is a resident of both Contracting States, a series of tie-breaker rules are provided in paragraph 2 to determine a single State of residence for that individual. These tests are to be applied in the order in which they are stated. The first test is based on where the individual has a permanent home. If that test is inconclusive because the individual has a permanent home available to him in both States, he will be considered to be a resident of the Contracting State where his personal and economic relations are closest (*i.e.*, the location of his "center of vital interests"). If that test is also inconclusive, or if he does not have a permanent home available to him in either State, he will be treated as a resident of the Contracting State where he maintains a habitual abode. If he has a habitual abode in both States or in neither of them, he will be treated as a resident of the Contracting State of which he is a national. If he is a national of both States or of neither, competent authorities shall settle the question by mutual agreement.

Paragraph 3

Dual residents other than individuals (such as companies, trusts or estates) are addressed by paragraph 3. If such a person is, under the rules of paragraph 1, resident in both Contracting States, the competent authorities shall seek to determine a single State of residence for that person for purposes of the Convention. If the competent authorities are unable to reach such an agreement, that person may not claim any benefit provided by the Convention, except for those provided by Article 26 (Mutual Agreement Procedure).

Regardless of the outcomes under this paragraph, dual resident companies, may be treated as resident of a Contracting State for purposes other than that of obtaining benefits under the Convention. For example, if a dual resident company pays a dividend to a resident of Chile, the U.S. paying agent would withhold on that dividend at the appropriate treaty rate because reduced withholding is a benefit enjoyed by the resident of Chile, not by the dual resident company. The dual resident company that paid the dividend would, for this purpose, be treated as a resident of the United States under the Convention. In addition, information relating to dual resident persons can be exchanged under the Convention because, by its terms, Article 27 (Exchange of Information) is not limited to residents of the Contracting States.

ARTICLE 5 (PERMANENT ESTABLISHMENT)

This Article defines the term "permanent establishment," a term that is significant for several articles of the Convention. The existence of a permanent establishment in a Contracting State is necessary under Article 7 (Business Profits) for the taxation by that State of the business profits of a resident of the other Contracting State. Articles 10 (Dividends), 11 (Interest), and 12 (Royalties) provide for reduced rates of tax at source on payments of these items of income to a resident of the other State only when the income is not attributable to a permanent establishment that the recipient has in the source State. The concept is also relevant in determining which Contracting State may tax certain gains under Article 13 (Capital Gains) and certain "other income" under Article 21 (Other Income).

Paragraph 1

The basic definition of the term "permanent establishment" is contained in paragraph 1. As used in the Convention, the term means a fixed place of business through which the business of an enterprise is wholly or partly carried on. As indicated in the OECD Commentary to Article 5 (see paragraphs 4 through 8), a general principle to be observed in determining whether a permanent establishment exists is that the place of business must be "fixed" in the sense that a particular building or physical location is used by the enterprise for the conduct of its business, and that it must be foreseeable that the enterprise's use of this building or other physical location will be more than temporary.

Paragraph 2

Paragraph 2 lists a number of types of fixed places of business that constitute a permanent establishment. This list is illustrative and non-exclusive. According to paragraph 2, the term permanent establishment includes a place of management, a branch, an office, a factory, a workshop, and a mine, oil or gas well, quarry or any other place of extraction or exploitation of natural resources.

Paragraph 3

Subparagraphs 3(a) and 3(b) provide rules to determine whether a building site or a construction, assembly or installation project, or an installation or drilling rig or ship used for the exploration of natural resources constitutes a permanent establishment for the contractor, driller, etc. Subparagraph 3(a) provides that an installation used for on-land exploration of natural resources does not create a permanent establishment unless it lasts, or the activity continues, for more than three months. Subparagraph 3(b) provides that a building site or construction or installation project and the supervisory activities in connection therewith, or a drilling rig or ship used for the exploration of natural resources not referred to in subparagraph 3(a) does not create a permanent establishment unless it lasts, or the activity continues, for more than six months. It is only necessary to refer to "exploration" and not "exploitation" in this context because exploitation activities are defined to constitute a permanent establishment under subparagraph 2(f). Thus, a drilling rig does not constitute a permanent establishment if a well is drilled in only two months, but if production begins in the following month the well becomes a permanent establishment as of that date.

In applying subparagraphs 3(a) and 3(b), time spent by a sub-contractor on a building site is counted as time spent by the general contractor at the site for purposes of determining whether the general contractor has a permanent establishment. However, for the sub-contractor to be treated as having a permanent establishment, the sub-contractor's activities at the site must last for more than 12 months. If a sub-contractor is on a site intermittently, then, for purposes of applying the 12-month rule, time is measured from the first day the sub-contractor is on the site until the last day he is on the site (*i.e.*, intervening days that the sub-contractor is not on the site are counted).

Subparagraph 3(c) provides that an enterprise is deemed to have a permanent establishment in the other Contracting State if the enterprise performs services in that other State for a period or periods exceeding in the aggregate 183 days in any twelve month period, and these services are performed through one or more individuals who are present and performing such services in that other State. Subparagraph 3(c) applies only to the performance of services by an enterprise and only to services performed by an enterprise for third parties. Thus, the provision does not have the effect of deeming an enterprise to have a permanent establishment merely because services are provided to that enterprise. The provision only applies to services that are performed by an enterprise of a Contracting State within the other Contracting State. It is therefore not sufficient that the relevant services be merely furnished to a resident of the other Contracting State. Where, for example, an enterprise provides customer support or other services by telephone or computer to customers located in the other State, those would not be covered by subparagraph 3(c) because they are not performed by that enterprise within the other State. Another example would be that of an architect who is hired to design blueprints for the construction of a building in the other State. As part of completing the project, the architect must make visits to that other State, and his days of presence there would be counted for purposes of determining whether the 183-day threshold is satisfied. However, the days that the architect spends working on the blueprint in his home office shall not count for purposes of the 183-day threshold, because the architect is not performing those services within the other State.

Subparagraph 3(c) refers to days during which an enterprise performs services in the other Contracting State through one or more individuals who are present and performing such services in that other State. Accordingly, non-working days such as weekends or holidays would not count for purposes of the provision, as long as no services are actually being performed while in the other State on those days. For purposes of subparagraph 3(c), even if the enterprise sends many individuals simultaneously to the other State to provide services, their collective presence during one calendar day will count for only one day of the enterprise's presence in the other State. For instance, if an enterprise sends 20 employees to the other Contracting State to perform services for a client in that other State for 10 days, the enterprise will be considered to have performed services in that other State only for 10 days, not 200 days (20 employees x 10 days).

By deeming the enterprise to provide services through a permanent establishment in the other Contracting State, subparagraph 3(c) allows the application of Article 7 (Business Profits),

16

and accordingly, the taxation of the services shall be on a net basis. Such taxation is also limited to the profits attributable to the activities carried on in performing the relevant services. It will be important to ensure that only the profits properly attributable to the functions performed and risks assumed by provision of the services will be attributed to the deemed permanent establishment.

For purposes of computing the time limits described in paragraph 3, the time limits apply separately to each installation, site or project, as the case may be. The time period begins when work (including preparatory work carried on by the enterprise) physically begins in a Contracting State. A series of contracts or projects by a contractor that are interdependent both commercially and geographically are to be treated as a single project for purposes of applying the time period. For example, the construction of a housing development would be considered as a single project even if each house were constructed for a different purchaser.

If the relevant time limit is exceeded, the installation, site or project constitutes a permanent establishment from the first day of activity.

Paragraph 3 provides that for purposes of computing the time limits in paragraph 3, activities carried on by an enterprise associated with another enterprise, within the meaning of Article 9 (Associated Enterprises), shall be regarded as carried on by the last-mentioned enterprise if the activities of both enterprises are substantially the same, unless they are carried on simultaneously.

Paragraph 4

This paragraph contains exceptions to the general rule of paragraph 1, listing a number of activities that may be carried on through a fixed place of business but which nevertheless do not create a permanent establishment. The use of facilities solely to store, display or deliver merchandise belonging to an enterprise does not constitute a permanent establishment of that enterprise. The maintenance of a stock of goods belonging to an enterprise solely for the purpose of storage, display or delivery, or solely for the purpose of processing by another enterprise does not give rise to a permanent establishment of the first-mentioned enterprise. The maintenance of a fixed place of business solely for the purpose of purchasing goods or merchandise, or for collecting information, for the enterprise does not constitute a permanent establishment of that enterprise. The maintenance of a fixed place of business solely for the purpose of advertising, supplying information or carrying out scientific research for the enterprise or any other similar activity, if such activity is of a preparatory or auxiliary character does not constitute a permanent establishment of the enterprise.

Paragraph 5

Paragraphs 5 and 6 specify when activities carried on by an agent or other person acting on behalf of an enterprise create a permanent establishment of that enterprise. Under paragraph 5, a person is deemed to create a permanent establishment of the enterprise if that person has and habitually exercises an authority to conclude contracts that are binding on the enterprise. If, however, his activities are limited to those activities specified in paragraph 4 which would not constitute a permanent establishment if carried on by the enterprise through a fixed place of business, the person does not create a permanent establishment of the enterprise. For example, if the person has no authority to conclude contracts in the name of the enterprise with its customers for the sale of the goods produced by the enterprise, but it can enter into service contracts that are binding on the enterprise for the enterprise's business equipment, this contracting authority would not fall within the scope of the paragraph, even if exercised regularly.

The Convention uses the U.S. Model language "binding on the enterprise," rather than the OECD Model language "in the name of that enterprise." This difference in language is not intended to be a substantive difference. As indicated in paragraph 32 to the OECD Commentaries on Article 5, paragraph 5 of the Article is intended to encompass persons who have "sufficient authority to bind the enterprise's participation in the business activity in the State concerned."

Paragraph 6

Under paragraph 6, an enterprise is not deemed to have a permanent establishment in a Contracting State merely because it carries on business in that State through an independent agent, including a broker or general commission agent, if the agent is acting in the ordinary course of his business as an independent agent. Paragraph 8 of the Protocol identifies the two conditions that must be satisfied for a person to be within the scope of paragraph 6 of Article 5 of the Convention: the agent must be both legally and economically independent of the enterprise; and the agent must act in the ordinary course of its business in carrying out activities on behalf of the enterprise.

Whether the agent and the enterprise are independent is a factual determination. Among the questions to be considered is the extent to which the agent operates on the basis of instructions from the enterprise. An agent that is subject to (i) detailed instructions regarding the conduct of its operations, or (ii) comprehensive control by the enterprise is not legally independent.

In determining whether the agent is economically independent, a relevant factor is the extent to which the agent bears business risk. Business risk refers primarily to risk of loss. An independent agent typically bears risk of loss from its own activities. In the absence of other factors that would establish dependence, an agent that shares business risk with the enterprise, or has its own business risk, is economically independent because its business activities are not integrated with those of the principal. Conversely, an agent that bears little or no risk from the activities it performs is not economically independent and therefore is not described in paragraph 6.

Another relevant factor in determining whether an agent is economically independent is whether the agent acts exclusively or nearly exclusively for the principal. Such a relationship may indicate that the principal has economic control over the agent. A number of principals acting in concert also may have economic control over an agent. The limited scope of the agent's activities and the agent's dependence on a single source of income may indicate that the agent lacks economic independence. It should be borne in mind, however, that exclusivity is not in itself dispositive; an agent may be economically independent notwithstanding an exclusive relationship with the principal if it has the capacity to diversify and acquire other clients without substantial modifications to its current business and without substantial harm to its business profits. Thus, exclusivity should be viewed merely as a pointer to further investigation of the relationship between the principal and the agent. Each case must be addressed on the basis of its own facts and circumstances.

Paragraph 7

This paragraph clarifies that a company that is a resident of a Contracting State is not deemed to have a permanent establishment in the other Contracting State merely because it controls, or is controlled by, a company that is a resident of that other Contracting State, or that carries on business in that other Contracting State. The determination whether a permanent establishment exists is made solely on the basis of the factors described in paragraphs 1 through 6 of the Article. Whether a company is a permanent establishment of a related company, therefore, is based solely on those factors and not on the ownership or control relationship between the companies.

ARTICLE 6 (INCOME FROM REAL PROPERTY (IMMOVABLE PROPERTY))

This article deals with the taxation of income from real property (immovable property) situated in a Contracting State (the "situs State"). The Article does not grant an exclusive taxing right to the situs State; the situs State is merely given the primary right to tax. The Article does not impose any limitation in terms of rate or form of tax imposed by the situs State, except that, as provided in paragraph 9 of the Protocol, the situs State must allow the taxpayer an election to be taxed on a net basis.

Paragraph 1

The first paragraph of Article 6 states the general rule that income of a resident of a Contracting State derived from real property (immovable property) situated in the other Contracting State may be taxed in the Contracting State in which the property is situated. The paragraph specifies that income from real property (immovable property) includes income from agriculture and forestry. Given the availability of the net election in paragraph 9 of the Protocol, taxpayers generally should be able to obtain the same tax treatment in the situs country regardless of whether the income is treated as business profits or real property (immovable property) income.

Paragraph 2

The term "real property (immovable property)" is defined in paragraph 2 by reference to the internal law definition in the situs State. In the case of the United States, the term has the meaning given to it by Treas. Reg. § 1.897-1(b). In addition to the definitions in the two

Contracting States, the paragraph specifies certain additional classes of property that, regardless of domestic law definitions, are within the scope of the term for purposes of the Convention. This expanded definition conforms to that in the OECD Model. The definition of "real property (immovable property)" for purposes of Article 6 is more limited than the expansive definition of "real property (immovable property)" in paragraph 1 of Article 13 (Capital Gains). The Article 13 term includes not only real property (immovable property) as defined in Article 6 but certain other interests in real property (immovable property).

Paragraph 3

Paragraph 3 makes clear that all forms of income derived from the exploitation of real property (immovable property) are taxable in the Contracting State in which the property is situated. This includes income from any use of real property (immovable property), including, but not limited to, income from direct use by the owner (in which case income may be imputed to the owner for tax purposes) and rental income from the letting of real property (immovable property). In the case of a net lease of real property (immovable property), if a net election pursuant to paragraph 9 of the Protocol has not been made, the gross rental payment (before deductible expenses incurred by the lessee) is treated as income from the property.

Other income closely associated with real property (immovable property) is covered by other Articles of the Convention, however, and not Article 6. For example, income from the disposition of an interest in real property (immovable property) is not considered "derived" from real property (immovable property); taxation of that income is addressed in Article 13 (Capital Gains). Interest paid on a mortgage on real property (immovable property) property would be covered by Article 11 (Interest). Distributions by a U.S. Real Estate Investment Trust or certain regulated investment companies would fall under Article 13 in the case of distributions of U.S. real property gain or Article 10 (Dividends) in the case of distributions treated as dividends. Finally, distributions from a United States Real Property Holding Corporation are not considered to be income from the exploitation of real property (immovable property); such payments would fall under Article 10 or 13.

Paragraph 4

This paragraph specifies that the basic rule of paragraph 1 (as elaborated in paragraph 3) applies to income from real property (immovable property) of an enterprise and to income from real property (immovable property) used for the performance of independent personal services. This clarifies that the situs country may tax the real property income (including rental income) of a resident of the other Contracting State in the absence of attribution to a permanent establishment or a fixed base in the situs State. This provision represents an exception to the general rule under Articles 7 (Business Profits) and 14 (Independent Personal Services) that income must be attributable to a permanent establishment or fixed base in order to be taxable in the situs State.

Paragraph 9 of the Protocol

The paragraph provides that a resident of one Contracting State that derives real property (immovable property) income from the other State may elect, for any taxable year, to be subject to tax in that other State on a net basis, as though the income were attributable to a permanent establishment in that other State. In the case of real property (immovable property) situated in the United States, the election may be terminated only with the consent of the competent authority of the United States. Termination of such election will be granted in accordance with the provisions of Treas. Reg. § 1.871-10(d)(2).

The 2011 Exchange of Notes corrects a typographical error in the header of paragraph 9 of the Protocol. The header refers to paragraph 5 of Article 6. It should refer instead only to Article 6.

ARTICLE 7 (BUSINESS PROFITS)

This Article provides rules for the taxation by a Contracting State of the business profits of an enterprise of the other Contracting State.

Paragraph 1

Paragraph 1 states the general rule that business profits of an enterprise of one Contracting State may not be taxed by the other Contracting State unless the enterprise carries on business in that other Contracting State through a permanent establishment (as defined in Article 5 (Permanent Establishment)) situated there. When that condition is met, the State in which the permanent establishment is situated may tax the enterprise on the income that is attributable to the permanent establishment.

Because Article 7 applies to income earned by an enterprise from the furnishing of personal services, the article also applies to income derived by a partner resident in a Contracting State that is attributable to personal services performed in the other Contracting State through a partnership with a permanent establishment in that other State. Income which may be taxed under this Article includes all income attributable to the permanent establishment in respect of the performance of the personal services carried on by the partnership (whether by the partner himself, other partners in the partnership, or by employees assisting the partners) and any income from activities ancillary to the performance of those services (*e.g.*, charges for facsimile services).

The application of Article 7 to a service partnership may be illustrated by the following example. A partnership formed in Chile has five partners (who agree to split profits equally), four of whom are resident and perform personal services only in Chile at Office A, and one of whom performs personal services at Office B, a permanent establishment in the United States. In this case, the four partners of the partnership resident in Chile may be taxed in the United States in respect of their share of the income attributable to the permanent establishment, Office B. The services giving rise to income which may be attributed to the permanent establishment would include not only the services performed by the one resident partner, but also, for example, if one of the four other partners came to the United States and worked on an Office B matter

21

there, the income in respect of those services. Income from the services performed by the visiting partner would be subject to tax in the United States regardless of whether the visiting partner actually visited or used Office B while performing services in the United States.

Paragraph 2

Paragraph 2 provides rules for the attribution of business profits to a permanent establishment. The Contracting States will attribute to a permanent establishment the profits that it would have earned had it been a distinct and separate enterprise engaged in the same or similar activities under the same or similar conditions and dealing wholly independently with the enterprise of which it is a permanent establishment. This language incorporates the arm's-length standard for purposes of determining the profits attributable to a permanent establishment. The computation of business profits attributable to a permanent establishment under this paragraph is subject to the rules of paragraph 3 for the allowance of expenses incurred for the purposes of earning the profits.

The "attributable to" concept of paragraph 2 is analogous but not equivalent to the "effectively connected" concept in Code section 864(c). The profits attributable to a permanent establishment may be from sources within or without a Contracting State.

Paragraph 10 of the Protocol provides that the business profits attributed to a permanent establishment include only those derived from the assets or activities of the permanent establishment. This rule is consistent with the "asset-use" and "business activities" tests of Code section 864(c)(2).

Paragraph 3

Paragraph 3 provides that in determining the business profits of a permanent establishment, deductions shall be allowed for the necessary expenses incurred for the purposes of the permanent establishment, ensuring that business profits will be taxed on a net basis. This rule is not limited to expenses incurred exclusively for the purposes of the permanent establishment, but includes a reasonable allocation of executive and general administrative expenses, research and development expenses, interest, and other expenses incurred for the purposes of the enterprise as a whole, or that part of the enterprise that includes the permanent establishment, whether incurred in the Contracting State in which the permanent establishment is situated or elsewhere. Deductions are to be allowed regardless of which accounting unit of the enterprise books the expenses, so long as they are incurred for the purposes of the permanent establishment. For example, a portion of the interest expense recorded on the books of the home office in one State may be deducted by a permanent establishment in the other if properly allocable thereto. This rule permits (but does not require) each Contracting State to apply the type of expense allocation rules provided by U.S. law (such as in Treas. Reg. §§ 1.861-8 and 1.882-5).

Paragraph 3 does not permit a deduction for expenses charged to a permanent establishment by another unit of the enterprise. Thus, a permanent establishment may not deduct a royalty deemed paid to the head office. Similarly, a permanent establishment may not increase its business profits by the amount of any notional fees for ancillary services performed for another unit of the enterprise, but also should not receive a deduction for the expense of providing such services, since those expenses would be incurred for purposes of a business unit other than the permanent establishment.

Paragraph 4

Paragraph 4 provides that no business profits can be attributed to a permanent establishment merely because it purchases goods or merchandise for the enterprise of which it is a part. This rule applies only to an office that performs functions for the enterprise in addition to purchasing. The income attribution issue does not arise if the sole activity of the office is the purchase of goods or merchandise because such activity does not give rise to a permanent establishment under Article 5 (Permanent Establishment). A common situation in which paragraph 4 is relevant is one in which a permanent establishment purchases raw materials for the enterprise's manufacturing operation conducted outside the United States and sells the manufactured product. While business profits may be attributable to the permanent establishment with respect to its sales activities, no profits are attributable to it with respect to its purchasing activities.

Paragraph 5

Paragraph 5 provides that profits shall be determined by the same method each year, unless there is good reason to change the method used. This rule assures consistent tax treatment over time for permanent establishments. It limits the ability of both the Contracting State and the enterprise to change the accounting methods to be applied to the permanent establishment. It does not, however, restrict a Contracting State from imposing additional requirements, such as the rules under Code section 481, to prevent amounts from being duplicated or omitted following a change in accounting method.

Paragraph 6

Paragraph 6 coordinates the provisions of Article 7 and other provisions of the Convention. Under this paragraph, when business profits include items of income that are dealt with separately under other articles of the Convention, the provisions of those articles will, except when they specifically provide to the contrary, take precedence over the provisions of Article 7. For example, the taxation of dividends will be determined by the rules of Article 10 (Dividends), and not by Article 7, except where, as provided in paragraph 5 of Article 10, the dividend is attributable to a permanent establishment. In the latter case, the provisions of Article 7 apply. Thus, an enterprise of one State deriving dividends from the other State may not rely on Article 7 to exempt those dividends from tax at source if they are not attributable to a permanent establishment of the enterprise in the other State. By the same token, if the dividends are attributable to a permanent establishment in the other State, the dividends may be taxed on a net income basis at the source State's full corporate tax rate, rather than on a gross basis under Article 10.

As provided in Article 8 (International Transport), income derived from shipping and air transport activities in international traffic described in that Article is taxable only in the country of residence of the enterprise regardless of whether it is attributable to a permanent establishment situated in the source State.

Paragraph 7

Paragraph 7 incorporates into the Convention the rule of Code section 864(c)(6). Like the Code section on which it is based, paragraph 7 provides that any income or gain attributable to a permanent establishment or fixed base during its existence is taxable in the Contracting State where the permanent establishment or fixed base is situated, even if the payment of that income or gain is deferred until after the permanent establishment or fixed base ceases to exist. This rule applies with respect to this Article, paragraph 5 of Article 10 (Dividends), paragraph 6 of Article 11 (Interest), paragraph 4 of Article 12 (Royalties), paragraph 3 of Article 13 (Capital Gains), Article 14 (Independent Personal Services), and paragraph 2 of Article 21 (Other Income).

The effect of this rule can be illustrated by the following example. Assume a company that is a resident of the other Contracting State and that maintains a permanent establishment in the United States winds down the permanent establishment's business and sells the permanent establishment's inventory and assets to a U.S. buyer at the end of year 1 in exchange for an interest-bearing installment obligation payable in full at the end of year 3. Despite the fact that Article 13's threshold requirement for U.S. taxation is not met in year 3 because the company has no activities in the United States, the United States may tax the deferred income payment recognized by the company in year 3.

Paragraph 8

Paragraph 8 provides that notwithstanding the provisions of paragraph 1, in the absence of a permanent establishment, the United States may impose its excise tax on insurance premiums paid to foreign insurers, and Chile may impose its tax on payments for insurance policies contracted with foreign insurers. However, notwithstanding the provisions of Article 2 (Taxes Covered), such tax shall not exceed: (i) 2 percent of the gross amount of premiums in the case of policies of reinsurance; and (ii) 5 percent of the gross amount of premiums in the case of all other policies of insurance.

Paragraph 9

Paragraph 9 defines the term "business profits" to mean income from any trade or business. In accordance with this broad definition, the term "business profits" includes income attributable to notional principal contracts and other financial instruments to the extent that the income is attributable to a trade or business of dealing in such instruments or is otherwise related to a trade or business (as in the case of a notional principal contract entered into for the purpose of hedging currency risk arising from a trade or business). Any other income derived from such instruments is, unless specifically covered in another article, dealt with under Article 21 (Other Income).

In addition, the term includes income derived from the furnishing of personal services. Thus, a consulting firm resident in one State whose employees or partners perform services in the other State through a permanent establishment may be taxed in that other State on a net basis under Article 7, and not under Article 15 (Dependent Personal Services), which applies only to income of employees. With respect to the enterprise's employees themselves, however, their salary remains subject to Article 15.

Relationship to Other Articles

This Article is subject to the saving clause of paragraph 4 of the Protocol. Thus, if a citizen of the United States who is a resident of Chile under the Convention derives business profits from the United States that are not attributable to a permanent establishment in the United States, the United States may, subject to the special foreign tax credit rules of paragraph 3 of Article 23 (Relief from Double Taxation), tax those profits, notwithstanding the provision of paragraph 1 of this Article which would exempt the income from U.S. tax.

The benefits of this Article are also subject to Article 24 (Limitation on Benefits). Thus, an enterprise of Chile that derives income effectively connected with a U.S. trade or business may not claim the benefits of Article 7 unless the resident carrying on the enterprise qualifies for such benefits under Article 24.

ARTICLE 8 (INTERNATIONAL TRANSPORT)

This Article governs the taxation of profits from the operation of ships and aircraft in international traffic. The term "international traffic" is defined in subparagraph 1(g) of Article 3 (General Definitions).

Paragraph 1

Paragraph 1 provides that profits derived by an enterprise of a Contracting State from the operation in international traffic of ships or aircraft are taxable only in that Contracting State. Because paragraph 6 of Article 7 (Business Profits) defers to Article 8 with respect to shipping income, such income derived by a resident of one of the Contracting States may not be taxed in the other State even if the enterprise has a permanent establishment in that other State. Thus, if a U.S. airline has a ticket office in Chile, Chile may not tax the airline's profits attributable to that office under Article 7. Since entities engaged in international transportation activities normally will have many permanent establishments in a number of countries, the rule avoids difficulties that would be encountered in attributing income to multiple permanent establishments if the income were covered by Article 7.

Paragraph 2

The profits from the operation of ships or aircraft in international traffic that is exempt from tax under paragraph 1 is defined in paragraph 2.

In addition to profits derived directly from the operation of ships or aircraft in international traffic, this definition also includes certain items of rental income. First, profits from the operation of ships or aircraft include profits of an enterprise of a Contracting State from the rental of ships or aircraft on a full (time or voyage) basis (*i.e.*, with crew). Therefore, such profits are exempt from tax in the other Contracting State under paragraph 1. Also, paragraph 2 encompasses profits from the charter or rental of ships or aircraft on a bareboat basis (*i.e.*, without crew) if those profits are incidental to profits from the operation by the enterprise of ships or aircraft in international traffic. If profits of an enterprise from bareboat rentals are not incidental to profits from that enterprise's operation of ships or aircraft in international traffic, the profits from the bareboat rentals would constitute business profits and would be taxed in accordance with the provisions of Article 7.

Paragraph 11 of the Protocol provides that inland transport within either Contracting State shall be treated as the operation of ships or aircraft in international traffic if undertaken as part of a transport that includes transport by ships or aircraft in international traffic. Thus, consistent with the Commentary to Article 8 of the OECD Model, profits of an enterprise from the inland transport of property or passengers within either Contracting State falls within Article 8 if the transport is undertaken as part of the international transport of property or passengers by the enterprise. For example, if a U.S. shipping company contracts to carry property from Chile to a U.S. city and, as part of that contract, it transports the property by truck from its point of origin to an airport in Chile (or it contracts with a trucking company to carry the property to the airport) the income earned by the U.S. shipping company from the overland leg of the journey would be taxable only in the United States. Similarly, Article 8 also would apply to all of the income derived from a contract for the international transport of goods, even if the goods were transported to the port by a lighter, not by the vessel that carried the goods in international waters.

Finally, certain non-transport activities that are an integral part of the services performed by a transport company, or are ancillary to the enterprise's operation of ships or aircraft in international traffic, are understood to be covered in paragraph 1, though they are not specified in paragraph 2. These include, for example, the provision of goods and services by engineers, ground and equipment maintenance and staff, cargo handlers, catering staff and customer services personnel. Where the enterprise provides such goods to, or performs services for, other enterprises and such activities are directly connected with or ancillary to the enterprise's operation of ships or aircraft in international traffic, the profits from the provision of such goods and services to other enterprises will fall under this paragraph.

For example, enterprises engaged in the operation of ships or aircraft in international traffic may enter into pooling arrangements for the purposes of reducing the costs of maintaining facilities needed for the operation of their ships or aircraft in other countries. For instance, where an airline enterprise agrees (for example, under an International Airlines Technical Pool agreement) to provide spare parts or maintenance services to other airlines landing at a particular location (which allows it to benefit from these services at other locations), activities carried on pursuant to that agreement will be ancillary to the operation of aircraft in international traffic by the enterprise.

Also, advertising that the enterprise may do for other enterprises in magazines offered aboard ships or aircraft that it operates in international traffic or at its business locations, such as ticket offices, is ancillary to its operation of these ships or aircraft. Profits generated by such advertising fall within this paragraph. Income earned by concessionaires, however, is not covered by Article 8. These interpretations of paragraph 1 also are consistent with the Commentary to Article 8 of the OECD Model.

Paragraph 3

Under this paragraph, profits of an enterprise of a Contracting State from the use, maintenance or rental of containers (including related equipment, such as barges and trailers, for the transport of such containers) used for the transport of goods or merchandise in international traffic are exempt from tax in the other Contracting State. This result obtains under paragraph 3 regardless of whether the recipient of the income is engaged in the operation of ships or aircraft in international traffic, and regardless of whether the enterprise has a permanent establishment in the other Contracting State. Only income from the use, maintenance or rental of containers that is incidental to other income from international traffic is covered by Article 8 of the OECD Model.

Paragraph 4

This paragraph clarifies that the provisions of paragraphs 1 and 3 also apply to profits of an enterprise of a Contracting State from participation in a pool, joint business or international operating agency. This refers to various arrangements for international cooperation by carriers in shipping and air transport. For example, airlines from two countries may agree to share the transport of passengers between the two countries. They each will fly the same number of flights per week and share the revenues from that route equally, regardless of the number of passengers that each airline actually transports. Paragraph 4 makes clear that with respect to each carrier the income dealt with in the Article is that carrier's share of the total transport, not the income derived from the passengers actually carried by the airline. This paragraph corresponds to paragraph 4 of Article 8 of the OECD Model.

Relationship to Other Articles

The taxation of gains from the alienation of ships, aircraft or containers is not dealt with in this Article but in paragraph 4 of Article 13 (Capital Gains).

As with other benefits of the Convention, the benefit of exclusive residence country taxation under Article 8 is available to an enterprise only if it is entitled to benefits under Article 24 (Limitation on Benefits).

This Article also is subject to the saving clause of paragraph 4 of the Protocol. Thus, if a citizen of the United States who is a resident of Chile derives profits from the operation of ships or aircraft in international traffic, notwithstanding the exclusive residence country taxation in paragraph 1 of Article 8, the United States may, subject to the special foreign tax credit rules of paragraph 3 of Article 23 (Relief from Double Taxation), tax those profits as part of the worldwide income of the citizen. (This is an unlikely situation, however, because non-tax considerations (*e.g.*, insurance) generally result in shipping activities being carried on in corporate form.)

ARTICLE 9 (ASSOCIATED ENTERPRISES)

This Article incorporates into the Convention the arm's-length principle reflected in the U.S. domestic transfer pricing provisions, particularly Code section 482. It provides that when related enterprises engage in a transaction on terms that are not arm's-length, the Contracting States may make appropriate adjustments to the taxable income and tax liability of such related enterprises to reflect what the income and tax of these enterprises with respect to the transaction would have been had there been an arm's-length relationship between them.

Paragraph 1

This paragraph addresses the situation where an enterprise of a Contracting State is related to an enterprise of the other Contracting State, and there are arrangements or conditions imposed between the enterprises in their commercial or financial relations that are different from those that would have existed in the absence of the relationship. Under these circumstances, the Contracting States may adjust the income (or loss) of the enterprise to reflect what it would have been in the absence of such a relationship.

The paragraph identifies the relationships between enterprises that serve as a prerequisite to application of the Article. As the Commentary to the OECD Model makes clear, the necessary element in these relationships is effective control, which is also the standard for purposes of section 482. Thus, the Article applies if an enterprise of one State participates directly or indirectly in the management, control, or capital of the enterprise of the other State. Also, the Article applies if any third person or persons participate directly or indirectly in the management, control, or capital of enterprises of different States. For this purpose, all types of control are included, *i.e.*, whether or not legally enforceable and however exercised or exercisable.

The fact that a transaction is entered into between such related enterprises does not, in and of itself, mean that a Contracting State may adjust the income (or loss) of one or both of the enterprises under the provisions of this Article. If the conditions of the transaction are consistent with those that would be made between independent persons, the income arising from that trans-action should not be subject to adjustment under this Article.

Similarly, the fact that associated enterprises may have concluded arrangements, such as cost sharing arrangements or general services agreements, is not in itself an indication that the two enterprises have entered into a non-arm's-length transaction that should give rise to an adjustment under paragraph 1. Both related and unrelated parties enter into such arrangements (*e.g.*, joint venturers may share some development costs). As with any other kind of transaction, when related parties enter into an arrangement, the specific arrangement must be examined to see whether or not it meets the arm's-length standard. In the event that it does not, an appropriate adjustment may be made, which may include modifying the terms of the agreement or re-characterizing the transaction to reflect its substance.

It is understood that the "commensurate with income" standard for determining appropriate transfer prices for intangibles, added to Code section 482 by the Tax Reform Act of 1986, was designed to operate consistently with the arm's-length standard. The implementation of this standard in the section 482 regulations is in accordance with the general principles of paragraph 1 of Article 9 of the Convention, as interpreted by the OECD Transfer Pricing Guidelines.

This Article also permits tax authorities to deal with thin capitalization issues. They may, in the context of Article 9, scrutinize more than the rate of interest charged on a loan between related persons. They also may examine the capital structure of an enterprise, whether a payment in respect of that loan should be treated as interest, and, if it is treated as interest, under what circumstances interest deductions should be allowed to the payor. Paragraph 2 of the Commentary to Article 9 of the OECD Model, together with the U.S. observation set forth in paragraph 15, sets forth a similar understanding of the scope of Article 9 in the context of thin capitalization.

Paragraph 2

When a Contracting State has made an adjustment that is consistent with the provisions of paragraph 1, and the other Contracting State agrees that the adjustment was appropriate to reflect arm's-length conditions, that other Contracting State is obligated to make a correlative adjustment (sometimes referred to as a "corresponding adjustment") to the tax liability of the related person in that other Contracting State. Although the OECD Model does not specify that the other Contracting State must agree with the initial adjustment before it is obligated to make the correlative adjustment, the Commentary makes clear that the paragraph is to be read that way.

As explained in the Commentary to Article 9 of the OECD Model, Article 9 leaves the treatment of "secondary adjustments" to the laws of the Contracting States. When an adjustment under Article 9 has been made, one of the parties will have in its possession funds that it would not have had at arm's length. The question arises as to how to treat these funds. In the United States, the general practice is to treat such funds as a dividend or contribution to capital, depending on the relationship between the parties. Under certain circumstances, the parties may be permitted to restore the funds to the party that would have the funds had the transactions been entered into on arm's length terms, and to establish an account payable pending restoration of the funds. *See* Rev. Proc. 99-32, 1999-2 C.B. 296.

The Contracting State making a secondary adjustment will take the other provisions of the Convention, where relevant, into account. For example, if the effect of a secondary adjustment is to treat a U.S. corporation as having made a distribution of profits to its parent corporation in Chile, the provisions of Article 10 (Dividends) will apply, and the United States may impose a 5 percent withholding tax on the dividend. Also, if under Article 23 (Relief from Double Taxation) Chile generally gives a credit for taxes paid with respect to such dividends, it would also be required to do so in this case.

The competent authorities are authorized by paragraph 3 of Article 26 (Mutual Agreement Procedure) to consult, if necessary, to resolve any differences in the application of these provisions. For example, there may be a disagreement over whether an adjustment made by a Contracting State under paragraph 1 was appropriate.

If a correlative adjustment is made under paragraph 2, it is to be implemented, pursuant to paragraph 2 of Article 26 (Mutual Agreement Procedure), notwithstanding any time limits or other procedural limitations in the law of the Contracting State making the adjustment. Thus, even if a statute of limitations has run, a refund of tax can be made in order to implement a correlative adjustment (statutory or procedural limitations , however, cannot be overridden to impose additional tax, because paragraph 2 of Article 1 (General Scope) provides that the Convention cannot restrict any statutory benefit). If a taxpayer has entered a closing agreement (or other written settlement) with the United States prior to bringing a case to the competent authorities, the U.S. competent authority will endeavor only to obtain a correlative adjustment from Chile. *See* Rev. Proc. 2006-54, 2006-2 C.B. 1035, § 7.05 (or any applicable successor procedures).

Relationship to Other Articles

The saving clause of paragraph 4 of the Protocol does not apply to paragraph 2 of Article 9 by virtue of an exception to the saving clause in subparagraph 4(a) of the Protocol. This ensures that the competent authorities of the Contracting States have the ability to make any adjustments necessary to relieve double taxation pursuant to the mutual agreement procedure.

ARTICLE 10 (DIVIDENDS)

Article 10 provides rules for the taxation of dividends paid by a company that is a resident of one Contracting State to a beneficial owner that is a resident of the other Contracting State. The Article provides for full residence-State taxation of such dividends and a limited source-State right to tax. Article 10 also provides rules for the imposition of a tax on branch profits by the State of source. Finally, the Article prohibits a State from imposing taxes on a company resident in the other Contracting State, other than a branch profits tax, on undistributed earnings.

Paragraph 1

Paragraph 1 permits a Contracting State to tax its residents on dividends paid to them by a company that is a resident of the other Contracting State. For dividends from any other source paid to a resident, Article 21 (Other Income) grants the State of residence exclusive taxing jurisdiction (other than for dividends attributable to a permanent establishment in the other State).

Paragraph 2

The State of source also may tax dividends beneficially owned by a resident of the other State, subject to the limitations of paragraphs 2 and 3. Paragraph 2 generally limits the rate of withholding tax in the State of source on dividends paid by a company resident in that State to 15 percent of the gross amount of the dividend. If, however, the beneficial owner of the dividend is a company resident in the other State and owns directly shares representing at least 10 percent of the voting stock of the company paying the dividend, then the rate of withholding tax is limited to 5 percent of the gross amount of the dividend. For application of this paragraph by the United States, shares are considered voting shares if they provide the power to elect, appoint or replace any person vested with the powers ordinarily exercised by the board of directors of a U.S. corporation.

The determination of whether the ownership threshold for subparagraph (a) is met for purposes of the 5 percent maximum rate of withholding tax is made on the date on which entitlement to the dividend is determined. Thus, the determination would generally be made on the dividend record date.

Paragraph 2 does not affect the taxation of the profits out of which the dividends are paid. The taxation by a Contracting State of the income of its resident companies is governed by the internal law of the Contracting State, subject to the provisions of paragraph 3 of Article 25 (Non-Discrimination).

The term "beneficial owner" is not defined in the Convention, and is, therefore, defined as under the internal law of the State granting treaty benefits (*i.e.*, the source State). The beneficial owner of the dividend for purposes of Article 10 is the person to which the income is attributable under the laws of the source State. Thus, if a dividend paid by a corporation that is a resident of one of the States (as determined under Article 4 (Residence)) is received by a nominee or agent that is a resident of the other State on behalf of a person that is not a resident of that other State, the dividend is not entitled to the benefits of this Article. However, a dividend received by a nominee on behalf of a resident of that other State would be entitled to benefits. These limitations are confirmed by paragraph 12 of the Commentary to Article 10 of the OECD Model. *See also* paragraph 24 of the Commentary to Article 1 of the OECD Model.

Special rules, however, apply to shares that are held through fiscally transparent entities. In that case, the rules of paragraph 1 of the Protocol will apply to determine whether the dividends should be treated as having been derived by a resident of a Contracting State. Residence-State principles shall be used to determine who derives the dividend, to assure that the dividends for which the source State grants benefits of the Convention will be taken into account for tax purposes by a resident of the residence State. Source-State principles of beneficial ownership shall then apply to determine whether the person who derives the dividends, or another resident of the other Contracting State, is the beneficial owner of the dividend. If the person who derives the dividend under paragraph 1 of the Protocol would not be treated as a nominee, agent, custodian, conduit, etc., under the source State's principles for determining beneficial ownership, that person will be treated as the beneficial owner of the income, profits or gains for purposes of the Convention.

Assume for instance, that a company resident in Chile pays a dividend to LLC, an entity that is treated as fiscally transparent for U.S. tax purposes but is treated as a company for Chilean tax purposes. USCo, a corporation incorporated in the United States, is the sole interest holder in LLC. Paragraph 1 of the Protocol provides that USCo derives the dividend. Chile's principles of beneficial ownership shall then be applied to USCo. If under the laws of Chile USCo is found not to be the beneficial owner of the dividend, USCo will not be entitled to the benefits of Article 10 with respect to such dividend. If USCo is found to be a nominee, agent, custodian, or conduit for another person who is a resident of the United States, that person may be entitled to benefits with respect to the dividends.

Beyond identifying the person to whom the principles of beneficial ownership shall be applied, the principles of paragraph 1 of the Protocol will also apply when determining whether other requirements, such as the ownership threshold of subparagraph 2(a) of Article 10 have been satisfied.

For example, assume that FCo, a corporation that is a resident of Chile, owns a 50 percent interest in FP, a partnership that is organized in Chile. FP owns 100 percent of the sole class of stock of USCo, a company resident in the United States. Chile views FP as fiscally transparent under its domestic law, and accordingly taxes FCo currently on its distributive share of the income of FP and determines the character and source of the income received through FP in the hands of FCo as if such income were realized directly by FCo. In this case, FCo is treated as deriving 50 percent of the dividends paid by USCo under paragraph 1 of the Protocol. Moreover, FCo is treated as owning 50 percent of the stock of USCo directly. The same result would be reached even if the tax laws of the United States would treat FP differently (*e.g.*, if FP were not treated as fiscally transparent in the United States), or if FP were organized in a third state, as long as FP were still treated as fiscally transparent under the laws of the other Contracting State. The same principles would apply in determining whether companies holding shares through other fiscally transparent entities such as partnerships, trusts, and estates would qualify for benefits. As a result, companies holding shares through such entities may be able to claim the benefits of subparagraph (a) under certain circumstances. The lower rate applies when the company's proportionate share of the shares held by the intermediate entity meets the 10 percent threshold, and the company meets the requirements of paragraph 1 of the Protocol (*i.e.*, the company's country of residence treats the intermediate entity as fiscally transparent) with respect to the dividend. Whether this ownership threshold is satisfied may be difficult to determine and often will require an analysis of the partnership or trust agreement.

Paragraph 3

Paragraph 3 provides that dividends beneficially owned by an entity that is established and maintained in a Contracting State principally to provide or administer pensions or other similar benefits to employed and self-employed persons, or to earn income for the benefit of one or more such arrangements, and that is generally exempt from tax in that State, may not be taxed in the other Contracting State of which the payer of the dividends is a resident, provided that such dividends are not derived from the carrying on of a trade or business, directly or indirectly, by the beneficial owner or through an associated enterprise.

Paragraph 4

Paragraph 4 defines the term dividends broadly and flexibly. The definition is intended to cover all arrangements that yield a return on an equity investment in a corporation as determined under the tax law of the state of source, as well as arrangements that might be developed in the future.

The term includes income from shares, or other corporate rights that are not treated as debt under the law of the source State, and that participate in the profits of the company. The term also includes income from rights that is subjected to the same tax treatment as income from shares by the law of the State of source. Thus, a constructive dividend that results from a non-arm's length transaction between a corporation and a related party is a dividend. In the case of the United States, the term dividend includes amounts treated as a dividend under U.S. law upon the sale or redemption of shares or upon a transfer of shares in a reorganization. *See, e.g.*, Rev. Rul. 92-85, 1992-2 C.B. 69 (sale of foreign subsidiary's stock to U.S. sister company is a deemed dividend to extent of the subsidiary's and sister company's earnings and profits). Further, a distribution from a U.S. publicly traded limited partnership, which is taxed as a corporation under U.S. law, is a dividend for purposes of Article 10. However, a distribution by a limited liability company is not taxable by the United States under Article 10, provided the limited liability company is not characterized as an association taxable as a corporation under U.S. law.

Finally, a payment denominated as interest may be treated as a dividend to the extent that the debt is re-characterized as equity under the laws of the source State.

Paragraph 5

Paragraph 5 provides a rule for taxing dividends attributable to a permanent establishment or fixed base. In such case, the rules of Article 7 (Business Profits) or Article 14 (Independent Personal Services), as the case may be, shall apply. Accordingly, the dividends will be taxed on a net basis using the rates and rules of taxation generally applicable to residents of the State in which the permanent establishment or fixed base is located, as such rules may be modified by the Convention. An example of dividends attributable to a permanent establishment would be dividends derived by a dealer in stock or securities from stock or securities that the dealer held for sale to customers.

Paragraph 6

The right of a Contracting State to tax dividends paid by a company that is a resident of the other Contracting State is restricted by paragraph 6 to cases in which the dividends are paid to a resident of that Contracting State or are attributable to a permanent establishment or fixed base in that Contracting State. Thus, a Contracting State may not impose a "secondary" withholding tax on dividends paid by a nonresident company out of earnings and profits from that Contracting State.

The paragraph also restricts the right of a Contracting State to impose corporate level taxes on undistributed profits, other than a branch profits tax. The paragraph does not restrict a State's right to tax its resident shareholders on undistributed earnings of a corporation resident in the other State. For example, the authority of the United States to impose taxes on subpart F income and on earnings deemed invested in U.S. property, and its tax on income of a passive foreign investment company that is a qualified electing fund is in no way restricted by this provision.

Paragraph 7

Paragraph 7 permits a Contracting State to impose a branch profits tax on a company resident in the other Contracting State. The tax is in addition to other taxes permitted by the Convention. The term "company" is defined in subparagraph 1(e) of Article 3 (General Definitions).

A Contracting State may impose a branch profits tax on a company if the company has income attributable to a permanent establishment in that Contracting State, derives income from real property (immovable property) in that Contracting State that is taxed on a net basis under Article 6 (Income from Real Property (Immovable Property)), or realizes gains taxable in that State under paragraph 1 of Article 13 (Capital Gains). In the case of the United States, the imposition of such tax is limited, however, to the portion of the aforementioned items of income that represents the amount of such income that is the "dividend equivalent amount." This is consistent with the relevant rules under the U.S. branch profits tax, and the term dividend equivalent amount is defined under U.S. law. The dividend equivalent amount is an amount for a particular year that is equivalent to the income described above that is included in the corporation's effectively connected earnings and profits for that year, after payment of the corporate tax under Articles 6 (Income from Real Property (Immovable Property), 7 (Business Profits) or 13 (Capital Gains), reduced for any increase in the corporation's U.S. net equity during the year or increased for any reduction in its U.S. net equity during the year. *See* Code section 884(b); Treas. Reg. § 1.884-1. U.S. net equity is U.S. assets less U.S. liabilities. *See* Code section 884(c); Treas. Reg. § 1.884-1.

The dividend equivalent amount for any year approximates the dividend that a U.S. branch office would have paid during the year if the branch had been operated as a separate U.S. subsidiary company. If in the future Chile also imposes a branch profits tax, the base of its tax must be limited to an amount that is analogous to the dividend equivalent amount.

As discussed in the explanation of Article 1 (General Scope), consistency principles prohibit a taxpayer from applying provisions of the Code and this Convention inconsistently. In the context of the branch profits tax, this consistency requirement means that if a Chilean company uses the principles of Article 7 to determine its U.S. taxable income then it must also use those principles to determine its dividend equivalent amount. Similarly, if the Chilean company instead uses the Code to determine its U.S. taxable income, it must also use the Code to determine its dividend equivalent amount. As in the case of Article 7, if a Chilean company, for example, does not from year to year consistently apply the Code or the Convention to determine its dividend equivalent amount, then the Chilean company must make appropriate adjustments or recapture amounts that would otherwise be subject to U.S. branch profits tax if it had consistently applied the Code or the Convention to determine its dividend equivalent amount from year to year.

Paragraph 8

Paragraph 8 provides that the branch profits tax shall not be imposed at a rate exceeding five percent. It is intended that paragraph 8 apply equally if a taxpayer determines its taxable income under the laws of a Contracting State or under the provisions of Article 7. For example, as discussed above, consistency principles require a Chilean company that determines its U.S. taxable income under the Code to also determine its dividend equivalent amount under the Code. In that case, paragraph 8 would apply even though the Chilean company did not determine its dividend equivalent amount using the principles of Article 7.

Paragraph 12 of the Protocol

As stated in paragraph 4 of the 2010 Exchange of Notes, at the time of the signing of the Convention, Chile has an integrated tax system pursuant to which it collects a total 35 percent tax on business profits imposed at two levels. First, business profits of companies resident in Chile are subject to the First Category Tax at a rate of 17 percent. Second, in the case of non-resident shareholders, distributions are subject to Additional Tax at a rate of 35 percent of the gross amount of the distribution. Nonresident shareholders are allowed a credit for the First Category Tax in computing their liability for the Additional Tax. The effective rate of Additional Tax after a credit for the First Category Tax is 18 percent.

Paragraph 12 of the Protocol reflects the unique operation of Chile's integrated tax system and is intended to prevent the avoidance of the Additional Tax. Accordingly, subparagraph (a) provides that paragraphs 2, 3, 7, and 8 of Article 10 (Dividends) do not limit Chile's application of the Additional Tax provided that under the domestic law of Chile the First Category Tax is fully creditable in computing the amount of Additional Tax to be paid. Accordingly, as long as Chile allows a credit for the full amount of First Category Tax in computing the amount of Additional Tax to be paid, the Convention does not require Chile to reduce the rate of Additional Tax withheld on dividends paid by companies resident in Chile and beneficially owned by residents of the United States.

As provided in subparagraph 12(b) of the Protocol, if Chile makes certain changes to the Additional Tax or First Category Tax, Chile's right to tax under Article 10 will be limited as described below.

First, clause (i) of subparagraph 12(b) of the Protocol provides that if at any time under the domestic law of Chile the First Category Tax ceases to be fully creditable in computing the amount of Additional Tax to be paid, the provisions of subparagraph 12(a) of the Protocol shall not apply. Accordingly, the amount of Additional Tax imposed by Chile will be limited by paragraphs 2, 3, 7, and 8 of Article 10 (Dividends).

Second, clause (ii) of subparagraph 12(b) of the Protocol provides that if under the domestic law of Chile the rate of Additional Tax exceeds 35 percent, the provisions of Article 10 will apply to both the United States and Chile, but the tax charged under subparagraphs 2(a) and 2(b) of Article 10 will not exceed 15 percent of the gross amount of dividends paid by a resident of a Contracting State and beneficially owned by a resident of the other Contracting State. In such case, Chile and the United States will be equally bound by the provisions of Article 10, and dividends paid by a company resident in a Contracting State and beneficially owned by a resident of the other Contracting State may be taxed in the first-mentioned State, however, the tax so charged shall not exceed 15 percent of the gross amount of the dividends, regardless of whether the beneficial owner is a company that owns directly 10 percent of the company paying the dividends. If the rate of Additional Tax exceeds 35 percent, clause (ii) of subparagraph 12(b) of the Protocol also provides that the Contracting States shall consult to reassess the balance of benefits of the Convention with a view to concluding a protocol to incorporate terms limiting the right of the source State to tax dividends under Article 10.

Paragraph 13 of the Protocol

Paragraph 13 of the Protocol provides that Article 10 (Dividends) shall not apply in the case of distributions or dividends paid by an enterprise when the investment is subject to a foreign investment contract under the Foreign Investment Statute (*DL 600*), as it may be amended from time to time without changing the general principles thereof.

Paragraph 14 of the Protocol

Paragraph 14 of the Protocol imposes limitations on the rate reductions provided by paragraph 2 in the case of dividends paid by a RIC or a REIT.

The first sentence of paragraph 14 provides that dividends paid by a RIC or a REIT are not eligible for the 5 percent rate of withholding tax of subparagraph 2(a) of Article 10 (Dividends).

The second sentence of paragraph 14 provides that the 15 percent maximum rate of withholding tax of subparagraph (b) of paragraph 2 of Article 10 (Dividends) applies to dividends paid by RICs.

The third sentence of paragraph 14 provides that the 15 percent rate of withholding tax also applies to dividends paid by a REIT, provided that one of the three following conditions is met. First, the beneficial owner of the dividend is an individual holding an interest of not more than 10 percent in the REIT. Second, the dividend is paid with respect to a class of stock that is publicly traded and the beneficial owner of the dividend is a person holding an interest of not more than 5 percent of any class of the REIT's shares. Third, the beneficial owner of the dividend holds an interest in the REIT of not more than 10 percent and the REIT is "diversified."

Paragraph 14 provides a definition of the term diversified. A REIT is diversified if the gross value of no single interest in real property held by the REIT exceeds 10 percent of the gross value of the REIT's total interest in real property. Foreclosure property is not considered an interest in real property, and a REIT holding a partnership interest is treated as owning its proportionate share of any interest in real property held by the partnership.

Relationship to Other Articles

Notwithstanding the foregoing limitations on source country taxation of dividends, the saving clause of paragraph 4 of the Protocol permits the United States to tax dividends received by its residents and citizens, subject to the special foreign tax credit rules of paragraph 3 of Article 23 (Relief from Double Taxation), as if the Convention had not come into effect.

The benefits of this Article are also subject to the provisions of Article 24 (Limitation on Benefits). Thus, if a resident of the other Contracting State is the beneficial owner of dividends paid by a U.S. corporation, the shareholder must qualify for treaty benefits under at least one of the tests of Article 24 in order to receive the benefits of this Article.

ARTICLE 11 (INTEREST)

Article 11 provides rules for the taxation of interest arising in one Contracting State and paid to a beneficial owner that is a resident of the other Contracting State.

Paragraph 1

Paragraph 1 grants to the State of residence the non-exclusive right to tax interest beneficially owned by its residents and arising in the other Contracting State.

Paragraph 2

Paragraph 2 provides that the State of source also may tax interest beneficially owned by a resident of the other Contracting State, but generally limits the rate of tax to 10 percent of the gross amount of the interest. However, the rate of tax is limited to 4 percent of the gross amount of the interest if the beneficial owner of the interest is a resident of the other Contracting State that is: (1) a bank; (2) an insurance company; (3) an enterprise substantially deriving its gross income from the active and regular conduct of a lending or finance business involving transactions with unrelated parties, where the enterprise is unrelated to the payer of the interest; (4) an enterprise that sold machinery or equipment, where the interest is paid in connection with the sale on credit of such machinery or equipment; or (5) any other enterprise, provided that in the three tax years preceding the tax year in which the interest is paid, the enterprise derives more than 50 percent of its liabilities from the issuance of bonds in the financial markets or from taking deposits at interest, and more than 50 percent of the assets of the enterprise consist of debt-claims against persons that do not have with the resident a relationship described in subparagraph (a) or (b) of paragraph 1 of Article 9 (Associated Enterprises).

For purposes of subparagraph 2(a)(iii), under which certain enterprises substantially deriving their gross income from the active and regular conduct of a lending or finance business may qualify for the 4 percent rate, the term "lending or finance business" is defined to include the business of issuing letters of credit or providing guarantees, or providing charge and credit card services.

The term "beneficial owner" is not defined in the Convention, and is therefore defined under the internal law of the State granting treaty benefits (*i.e.*, the source State). The beneficial owner of the interest for purposes of Article 11 is the person to which the income is attributable under the laws of the source State. Thus, if interest arising in a Contracting State is received by a nominee or agent that is a resident of the other State on behalf of a person that is not a resident of that other State, the interest is not entitled to the benefits of Article 11. However, interest received by a nominee on behalf of a resident of that other State would be entitled to benefits. These limitations are similar to those provided in paragraph 9 of the OECD Commentary to Article 11.

Special rules apply to interest derived through fiscally transparent entities for purposes of determining the beneficial owner of the interest. In such cases, residence-State principles shall be used to determine who derives the interest, to assure that the interest for which the source State grants benefits of the Convention will be taken into account for tax purposes by a resident of the residence State.

For example, assume that FCo, a corporation that is a resident of Chile, owns a 50 percent interest in FP, a partnership that is organized in Chile. FP receives interest arising in the United States. Chile views FP as fiscally transparent under its domestic law, and thus taxes FCo currently on its distributive share of the income of FP and determines the character and source of the income received through FP in the hands of FCo as if such income were realized directly by FCo. In this case, FCo is treated as deriving 50 percent of the interest received by FP that arises in the United States under paragraph 1 of the Protocol. The same result would be reached even if the tax laws of the United States would treat FP differently (*e.g.*, if FP were not treated as fiscally transparent in the United States), or if FP were organized in a third state, as long as FP were still treated as fiscally transparent under the laws of Chile.

While residence-State principles control who is treated as deriving the interest, source-State principles of beneficial ownership apply to determine whether the person who derives the interest or another resident of the other Contracting State is the beneficial owner of the interest.

If the person who derives the interest under paragraph 1 of the Protocol would not be treated as a nominee, agent, custodian, conduit, etc., under the source State's principles for determining beneficial ownership, that person will be treated as the beneficial owner of the interest for purposes of the Convention. In the example above, FCo is required to satisfy the beneficial ownership principles of the United States with respect to the interest it derives. If under the beneficial ownership principles of the United States, FCo is found not to be the beneficial owner of the interest, FCo will not be entitled to the benefits of Article 11 with respect to such interest. If FCo is found to be a nominee, agent, custodian, or conduit for a person who is a resident of the other Contracting State, that person may be entitled to benefits with respect to the interest.

Paragraph 3

Paragraph 3 provides that the rate limitation of subparagraph 2(b) will be phased in. For five years from the date on which the provisions of paragraph 2 take effect, the rate of 15 percent will apply in lieu of the rate provided in subparagraph 2(b). Thereafter, the 10 percent rate will apply.

In addition, paragraph 22 of the Protocol provides that, if Chile concludes with another state an income tax treaty that imposes a limit on rates of withholding on payments of interest lower than the limits imposed under paragraph 2 of Article 11, the United States and Chile shall, at the request of the United States, consult to reassess the balance of benefits of the Convention with a view to concluding a protocol incorporating such lower rates into the Convention.

Paragraph 4

Paragraph 4 provides an anti-abuse exception to subparagraph 2(a). Interest described in that subparagraph may be taxed by the source State at a rate not exceeding 10 percent of the gross amount of the interest if the interest is paid as part of an arrangement involving back-to-back loans or another arrangement that is economically equivalent to and intended to have a similar effect as back-to-back loans. By referencing arrangements that are economically similar to and that have the effect of a back-to-back loan, paragraph 4 applies to transactions that would not meet the legal requirements of a loan but would nevertheless serve that purpose economically. For example, the term would encompass securities issued at a discount or certain swap arrangements intended to operate as the economic equivalent of a back-to-back loan.

Paragraph 5

The term "interest" as used in Article 11 is defined in paragraph 5 to include, *inter alia*, income from debt claims of every kind, whether or not secured by a mortgage. Penalty charges for late payment are excluded from the definition of interest. Interest that is paid or accrued subject to a contingency is within the ambit of Article 11. This definition includes income from a debt obligation carrying the right to participate in profits if the contract by its character clearly evidences a loan at interest. The term does not, however, include amounts treated as dividends under Article 10 (Dividends).

The term "interest" also includes amounts subject to the same tax treatment as income from money lent under the law of the State in which the income arises. Thus, for purposes of the Convention, amounts that the United States will treat as interest include: (i) the difference between the issue price and the stated redemption price at maturity of a debt instrument (*i.e.*, original issue discount ("OID")), which may be wholly or partially realized on the disposition of a debt instrument (section 1273); (ii) amounts that are imputed interest on a deferred sales contract (section 483); (iii) amounts treated as interest or OID under the stripped bond rules (section 1286); (iv) amounts treated as original issue discount under the below-market interest rate rules (section 7872); (v) a partner's distributive share of a partnership's interest income (section 702); (vi) the interest portion of periodic payments made under a "finance lease" or similar contractual arrangement that in substance is a borrowing by the nominal lessee to finance the acquisition of property; (vii) amounts included in the income of a holder of a residual interest in a REMIC (section 860E), because these amounts generally are subject to the same taxation treatment as interest under U.S. tax law; and (viii) interest with respect to notional principal contracts that are re-characterized as loans because of a "substantial non-periodic payment."

Paragraph 6

Paragraph 6 provides a rule for taxing interest in cases where the beneficial owner of the interest either carries on business through a permanent establishment in the other Contracting State, in which the interest arises, or performs in that other State independent personal services from a fixed base in that other State, and the interest is attributable to that permanent establishment or fixed base. In such cases the provisions of Article 7 (Business Profits) or 14 (Independent Personal Services), as the case may be, will apply, and the State of source will retain the right to impose tax on such interest income.

In the case of a permanent establishment or fixed base that once existed in the State of source but that no longer exists, the provisions of paragraph 6 also apply, by virtue of paragraph 7 of Article 7, to interest that would be attributable to such a permanent establishment or fixed base if it did exist in the year of payment or accrual. *See* the Technical Explanation of paragraph 7 of Article 7.

Paragraph 7

Paragraph 7 provides a source rule for interest that is identical in substance to the interest source rule of the OECD Model. Interest is considered to arise in a Contracting State if paid by a resident of that State. As an exception, interest on a debt incurred in connection with a permanent establishment or a fixed base in one of the States and borne by the permanent establishment or fixed base is deemed to arise in that State. For this purpose, interest is considered to be borne by a permanent establishment or fixed base if it is allocable to taxable income of that permanent establishment or fixed base.

Paragraph 8

Paragraph 8 provides that in cases involving special relationships between the payor and the beneficial owner of interest income, Article 11 applies only to that portion of the total interest payments that would have been made absent such special relationships (*i.e.*, an arm's-length interest payment). Any excess amount of interest paid remains taxable according to the laws of the United States and Chile, respectively, with due regard to the other provisions of the Convention. Thus, if the excess amount would be treated under the source country's law as a distribution of profits by a corporation, such amount could be taxed as a dividend rather than as interest, but the tax would be subject, if appropriate, to the rate limitations of paragraph 2 of Article 10 (Dividends).

The term "special relationship" is not defined in the Convention. In applying this paragraph, the United States considers the term to include the relationships described in Article 9, which in turn corresponds to the definition of "control" for purposes of Code section 482.

This paragraph does not address cases where, owing to a special relationship between the payer and the beneficial owner or between both of them and some other person, the amount of the interest is less than an arm's-length amount. In those cases a transaction may be characterized to reflect its substance and interest may be imputed consistent with the definition of "interest" in paragraph 5. For example, the United States would apply Code section 482 or 7872 to determine the amount of imputed interest in those cases.

Paragraph 9

Paragraph 9 provides anti-abuse exceptions to paragraph 2 for two classes of interest payments.

The first class of interest, dealt with in subparagraph 9(a), is so-called contingent interest. Under this provision, interest arising in one of the Contracting States that is determined with reference to receipts, sales, income, profits or other cash flows of the debtor or a related person, to any change in the value of any property of the debtor or a related person or to any dividend, partnership distribution or similar payment made by the debtor or a related person also may be taxed in the State in which it arises, and according to the laws of that State. If the beneficial owner is a resident of the other Contracting State, however, the gross amount of the interest may be taxed at a rate not exceeding the rate prescribed in subparagraph 2(b) of Article 10 (Dividends).

The second class of interest that is dealt with in subparagraph 9(b) is excess inclusions from U.S. real estate mortgage investment conduits ("REMICs"). Subparagraph 9(b) serves as a backstop to Code section 860G(b). That section generally requires that a foreign person holding a residual interest in a REMIC take into account for U.S. tax purposes "any excess inclusion" and "amounts includible … [under the REMIC provisions] when paid or distributed (or when the interest is disposed of)…."

Without a full tax at source, non-U.S. transferees of residual interests would have a competitive advantage over U.S. transferees at the time these interests are initially offered. Absent this rule, the United States would suffer a revenue loss with respect to mortgages held in a REMIC because of opportunities for tax avoidance created by differences in the timing of taxable and economic income produced by such interests. In many cases, the transfer to the foreign person is simply disregarded under Treas. Reg. § 1.860G-3. Subparagraph 9(b) also serves to indicate that excess inclusions from REMICs are not considered "other income" subject to Article 21 (Other Income) of the Convention.

Paragraph 10

Paragraph 10 permits a Contracting State to impose its branch level interest tax on a company resident in the other Contracting State. The base of this tax is the excess, if any, of the interest allocable to the profits of the company that are either attributable to a permanent establishment in the first-mentioned State (including gains under paragraph 3 of Article 13 (Capital Gains)) or subject to tax in the first-mentioned State under Article 6 (Income from Real Property (Immovable Property)) or paragraph 1 of Article 13 (Capital Gains)) over the interest paid by the permanent establishment, or in the case of profits subject to tax under Article 6 or Article 13(1), over the interest paid by that trade or business in the first-mentioned State. Such excess interest may be taxed as if it were interest arising in the first-mentioned State and beneficially owned by the resident of the other State. Thus, such excess interest may be taxed by the first-mentioned State at a rate not to exceed the applicable rates provided in paragraph 2.

Relationship to Other Articles

Notwithstanding the foregoing limitations on source country taxation of interest, the saving clause of paragraph 4 of the Protocol permits the United States to tax its residents and citizens, subject to the special foreign tax credit rules of paragraph 3 of Article 23 (Relief from Double Taxation), as if the Convention had not come into force.

As with other benefits of the Convention, the benefits of Article 11 are available to a resident of the other State only if that resident is entitled to those benefits under the provisions of Article 24 (Limitation on Benefits).

ARTICLE 12 (ROYALTIES)

Article 12 provides rules for the taxation of royalties arising in one Contracting State and paid to a beneficial owner that is a resident of the other Contracting State.

Paragraph 1

Paragraph 1 grants to the State of residence the non-exclusive right to tax royalties paid to its residents and arising in the other Contracting State.

Paragraph 2

Paragraph 2 provides that the State of source also may tax royalties, but if the beneficial owner of the royalties is a resident of the other Contracting State, the rate of tax shall be limited to 2 percent of the gross amount of the royalties described in subparagraph 3(a), and 10 percent of the gross amount of the royalties described in subparagraph 3(b).

The term "beneficial owner" is not defined in the Convention, and is, therefore, defined under the internal law of the State granting treaty benefits (*i.e.*, the source State). The beneficial owner of the royalty for purposes of Article 12 is the person to which the income is attributable under the laws of the source State. Thus, if a royalty arising in a Contracting State is received by a nominee or agent that is a resident of the other State on behalf of a person that is not a resident of that other State, the royalty is not entitled to the benefits of Article 12. However, a royalty received by a nominee on behalf of a resident of that other State would be entitled to benefits. These limitations are similar to those provided in paragraph 4 of the OECD Commentary to Article 12.

Special rules apply to royalties derived through fiscally transparent entities for purposes of determining the beneficial owner of the royalties. In such cases, residence-State principles shall be used to determine who derives the royalties to assure that the royalties for which the source State grants benefits of the Convention will be taken into account for tax purposes by a resident of the residence State.

For example, assume that FCo, a company that is a resident of Chile, owns a 50 percent interest in FP, a partnership that is organized in Chile. FP receives royalties arising in the United States. Chile views FP as fiscally transparent under its domestic law, and thus taxes FCo currently on its distributive share of the income of FP and determines the source and character of the income received through FP in the hands of FCo as if such income were realized directly by FCo. In this case, FCo is treated as deriving 50 percent of the royalties received by FP that arise in the United States under paragraph 1 of the Protocol. The same result would be reached even if the tax laws of the United States would treat FP differently (*e.g.*, if FP were not treated as fiscally transparent in the United States), or if FP were organized in a third state, as long as FP were still treated as fiscally transparent under the laws of Chile.

While residence-State principles control who is treated as deriving the royalties, source-State principles of beneficial ownership apply to determine whether the person who derives the royalties, or another resident of the other Contracting State, is the beneficial owner of the royalties. If the person who derives the royalties under paragraph 1 of the Protocol would not be treated as a nominee, agent, custodian, conduit, etc., under the source State's principles for determining beneficial ownership, that person will be treated as the beneficial owner of the royalties for purposes of the Convention. In the example above, FCo must satisfy the beneficial ownership principles of the United States with respect to the royalties it derives. If under the beneficial ownership principles of the United States, FCo is found not to be the beneficial owner of the royalties, FCo will not be entitled to the benefits of Article 12 with respect to such royalties. If FCo is found to be a nominee, agent, custodian, or conduit for a person who is a resident of the other Contracting State, that person may be entitled to benefits with respect to the royalties.

Paragraph 22 of the Protocol provides that, if Chile concludes with another state an income tax treaty that imposes a limit on withholding rates on payments of royalties that is lower than the limits imposed under paragraph 2 of Article 12, the United States and Chile shall, at the request of the United States, consult to reassess the balance of benefits of the Convention with a view to concluding a protocol incorporating such lower rates into the Convention.

Paragraph 3

Paragraph 3 defines the term "royalties" as used in Article 12, and the term "royalties" comprises two categories of consideration. The first category is any consideration for the use of, or the right to use, industrial, commercial or scientific equipment, but not including ships, aircraft or containers as dealt with in Article 8 (International Transport). The second category is any consideration for the use of, or the right to use, any copyright of literary, artistic, scientific or other work (including computer software, cinematographic films, audio or video tapes or disks, and other means of image or sound reproduction), any patent, trademark, design or model, plan, secret formula or process, or other like intangible property, or for information concerning industrial, commercial, or scientific experience. The second category also includes gain derived from the alienation of any property included in the second category, to the extent the gain is contingent on the productivity, use, or disposition of the property. Gains that are not so contingent are dealt with under Article 13 (Capital Gains).

For purposes of determining whether payments as consideration for computer software should be classified as royalties under Article 12, paragraph 16 of the Protocol provides that the paragraphs of the Commentary to Article 12 of the OECD Model Convention of 2008 addressing computer software (paragraphs 12 to 14.4 and paragraph 17 to 17.4) will apply.

The term "royalties" is defined in the Convention and therefore is generally independent of domestic law. Certain terms used in the definition are not defined in the Convention, but these may be defined under domestic tax law. For example, the term "secret process or formulas" is found in the Code, and its meaning has been elaborated in the context of sections 351 and 367. *See* Rev. Rul. 55-17, 1955-1 C.B. 388; Rev. Rul. 64-56, 1964-1 C.B. 133; Rev. Proc. 69-19, 1969-2 C.B. 301.

Consideration for the use or right to use cinematographic films, or works on film, tape, or other means of reproduction in radio or television broadcasting is specifically included in the definition of royalties. It is intended that, with respect to any subsequent technological advances in the field of radio or television broadcasting, consideration received for the use of such technology will also be included in the definition of royalties.

If an artist who is resident in one Contracting State records a performance in the other Contracting State, retains a copyrighted interest in a recording, and receives payments for the right to use the recording based on the sale or public playing of the recording, then the right of

44

such other Contracting State to tax those payments is governed by Article 12. *See* Boulez v. Commissioner, 83 T.C. 584 (1984), aff'd, 810 F.2d 209 (D.C. Cir. 1986). By contrast, if the artist earns in the other Contracting State income covered by Article 17 (Artistes and Sportsmen), for example, endorsement income from the artist's attendance at a film screening, and if such income also is attributable to one of the rights described in Article 12 (*e.g.*, the use of the artist's photograph in promoting the screening), Article 17 and not Article 12 is applicable to such income.

The term "industrial, commercial, or scientific experience" (sometimes referred to as "know-how") has the meaning ascribed to it in paragraph 11 *et seq.* of the Commentary to Article 12 of the OECD Model. Consistent with that meaning, the term may include information that is ancillary to a right otherwise giving rise to royalties, such as a patent or secret process.

Know-how also may include, in limited cases, technical information that is conveyed through technical or consultancy services. It does not include general educational training of the user's employees, nor does it include information developed especially for the user, such as a technical plan or design developed according to the user's specifications. Thus, as provided in paragraph 11.3 of the Commentary to Article 12 of the OECD Model, the term "royalties" does not include payments received as consideration for after-sales service, for services rendered by a seller to a purchaser under a warranty, or for pure technical assistance.

The term "royalties" also does not include payments for professional services (such as architectural, engineering, legal, managerial, medical or software development services). For example, income from the design of a refinery by an engineer (even if the engineer employed know-how in the process of rendering the design) or the production of a legal brief by a lawyer is not income from the transfer of know-how taxable under Article 12, but is income from services taxable under either Article 7 (Business Profits), 14 (Independent Personal Services) or 15 (Dependent Personal Services), as applicable. Professional services may be embodied in property that gives rise to royalties, however. Thus, if a professional contracts to develop patentable property and retains rights in the resulting property under the development contract, subsequent license payments made for those rights would be royalties.

Paragraph 4

This paragraph provides a rule for taxing royalties in cases where the beneficial owner of the royalties carries on business through a permanent establishment in the State of source or performs in the source State independent personal services from a fixed based therein, and the royalties are attributable to that permanent establishment or fixed base. In such cases the provisions of Article 7 or Article 14, as the case may be, will apply.

The provisions of paragraph 7 of Article 7 apply to this paragraph. For example, royalty income that is attributable to a permanent establishment and that accrues during the existence of the permanent establishment, but is received after the permanent establishment no longer exists, remains taxable under the provisions of Article 7, and not under this Article.

Paragraph 5

Paragraph 5 contains the source rule for royalties. Under subparagraph 5(a), royalties are treated as arising in a Contracting State when the payer is a resident of that State. Where, however, the payer, whether he is a resident of a Contracting State, has in a Contracting State a permanent establishment or fixed base in connection with which the liability to pay the royalties was incurred, and such royalties are borne by such permanent establishment or fixed base, then such royalties will be deemed to arise in the State in which the permanent establishment or fixed base is situated.

Subparagraph 5(b) provides that where a royalty is not treated as arising in a Contracting State under subparagraph 5(a), and the royalties are for the use of, or the right to use, in a Contracting State any property or right described in paragraph 3, then such royalties will be deemed to arise in that State and not in the State of which the payer is resident.

Paragraph 6

Paragraph 6 provides that in cases involving special relationships between the payer and beneficial owner of royalties or between both of them and some other person, Article 12 applies only to the extent the royalties would have been paid absent such special relationships (*i.e.*, an arm's-length royalty). Any excess amount of royalties paid remains taxable according to the laws of the two Contracting States, with due regard to the other provisions of the Convention. If, for example, the excess amount is treated as a distribution of corporate profits under domestic law, such excess amount will be taxed as a dividend rather than as royalties, but the tax imposed on the dividend payment will be subject to the rate limitations of paragraph 2 of Article 10 (Dividends).

Relationship to Other Articles

Notwithstanding the foregoing limitations on source State taxation of royalties, the saving clause of paragraph 4 of the Protocol permits the United States to tax its residents and citizens, subject to the special foreign tax credit rules of paragraph 3 of Article 23 (Relief from Double Taxation), as if the Convention had not come into force.

As with other benefits of the Convention, the benefits of Article 12 are available to a resident of the other State only if that resident is entitled to those benefits under Article 24 (Limitation on Benefits).

ARTICLE 13 (CAPITAL GAINS)

Article 13 assigns either primary or exclusive taxing jurisdiction over gains from the alienation of property to the State of residence or the State of source.

Paragraph 1

Paragraph 1 of Article 13 preserves the non-exclusive right of the State of source to tax gains attributable to the alienation of real property situated in that State. The paragraph therefore permits the United States to apply Code section 897 to tax gains derived by a resident of Chile that are attributable to the alienation of real property situated in the United States (as defined in paragraph 2). Gains attributable to the alienation of real property include gains from any other property that is treated as a real property interest within the meaning of paragraph 2.

Paragraph 1 refers to gains "attributable to the alienation of real property (immovable property)" rather than the OECD Model phrase "gains from the alienation" to clarify that the United States will look through distributions made by a REIT and certain RICs. Accordingly, distributions made by a REIT or certain RICs are taxable under paragraph 1 of Article 13 (not under Article 10 (Dividends)) when they are attributable to gains derived from the alienation of real property.

Paragraph 2

This paragraph defines the term "real property (immovable property) situated in the other Contracting State." The term includes real property (immovable property) referred to in Article 6 (Income from Real Property (Immovable Property)) (*i.e.*, an interest in the real property (immovable property) itself), a "United States real property interest" (when the United States is the other Contracting State under paragraph 1) as defined in Code section 897 and the regulations thereunder, as they may be amended from time to time without changing the general principles thereof, and an equivalent interest in real property (immovable property) situated in Chile, including shares or other rights deriving more than 50 percent of their value directly or indirectly from real property (immovable property) situated in Chile (when Chile is the other Contracting State under paragraph 1).

Under Code section 897(c) the term "United States real property interest" includes shares in a U.S. corporation that owns sufficient U.S. real property interests to satisfy an asset-ratio test on certain testing dates. The term also includes certain foreign corporations that have elected to be treated as U.S. corporations for this purpose. Section 897(i).

Paragraph 3

Paragraph 3 of Article 13 deals with the taxation of certain gains from the alienation of personal property (movable property) that are attributable to a permanent establishment that an enterprise of a Contracting State has in the other Contracting State, or that are attributable to a fixed base available to a resident of a Contracting State in the other Contracting State for the purpose of performing independent personal services. This also includes gains from the alien-ation of such a permanent establishment (alone or with the whole enterprise) or of the fixed base. Such gains may be taxed in the State in which the permanent establishment or fixed base is located.

A resident of Chile that is a partner in a partnership doing business in the United States generally will have a permanent establishment in the United States as a result of the activities of the partnership, assuming that the activities of the partnership rise to the level of a permanent establishment. *See* Unger v. Commissioner, 936 F.2d 1316 (D.C. Cir. 1991); Donroy, Ltd., v. United States, 301 F.2d 200 (9th Cir. 1962). *See also* Rev. Rul. 91-32, 1991-1 C.B. 107. Further, under paragraph 3, the United States generally may tax a partner's distributive share of income realized by a partnership on the disposition of movable property forming part of the business property of the partnership in the United States.

The gains subject to paragraph 3 may be taxed in the State in which the permanent establishment or fixed base is located, regardless of whether the permanent establishment or fixed base exists at the time of the alienation. This rule incorporates the rule of Code section 864(c)(6). Accordingly, income that is attributable to a permanent establishment or fixed base, but that is deferred and received after the permanent establishment or fixed base no longer exists, may nevertheless be taxed by the State in which the permanent establishment or fixed base was located.

Paragraph 4

This paragraph limits the taxing jurisdiction of the State of source with respect to gains from the alienation of ships, aircraft, or containers operated or used in international traffic and from personal property (movable property) pertaining to the operation or use of such ships, aircraft, or containers.

Under paragraph 4, such gains are taxable only in the Contracting State in which the alienator is resident. Notwithstanding paragraph 3, the rules of this paragraph apply even if the income is attributable to a permanent establishment or fixed base maintained by the enterprise in the other Contracting State. This result is consistent with the allocation of taxing rights under Article 8 (International Transport).

Paragraph 5

Paragraph 5 provides that gains derived by a resident of a Contracting State from the alienation of shares or other rights or interests representing the capital of a company that is a resident of the other Contracting State may be taxed in that other State, but the rate of tax shall be limited to 16 percent of the amount of the gain. As stated in paragraph 4 of the 2010 Exchange of Notes, the provisions of paragraph 5 (and paragraph 7, discussed below) of Article 13 reflect the unique operation of Chile's integrated tax system and are intended to prevent the avoidance of the Additional Tax.

Paragraph 16 of the Protocol provides that, if under the domestic law of Chile, the First Category Tax exceeds 30 percent, paragraph 5 (and paragraph 7, discussed below) of Article 13 shall not apply. In such case, paragraph 4 of the 2010 Exchange of Notes provides that paragraph 16 of the Protocol will operate to limit the right of the source State to tax capital gains, and such gains will only be subject to tax in the residence State.

Paragraph 22 of the Protocol provides that if Chile concludes with another state an income tax treaty that contains terms further limiting the right of the source State to tax capital gains under Article 13, the United States and Chile shall, at the request of the United States, consult to reassess the balance of benefits of the Convention with a view to concluding a protocol to incorporate such lower rates into the Convention.

Paragraph 6

Notwithstanding the provisions of paragraph 5, the State of residence of the alienator has the exclusive right to tax gains from the alienation of certain shares of a company or other rights representing the capital of a company that in either case is a resident of the other Contracting State as described in paragraph 6.

Gains derived by a pension fund from the alienation of shares or other rights representing the capital of a company that is a resident of the other Contracting State may be taxed only in the State of residence of the pension fund.

In addition, gains derived by a mutual fund or other institutional investor from the alienation of shares of a company that is a resident of the other Contracting State may be taxed only in the State of residence of the mutual fund or other institutional investor, provided that the company's shares are substantially and regularly traded on a recognized stock exchanged located in that other State and the alienation occurred on a recognized stock exchange in that other State. For this purpose, paragraph 17 of the Protocol provides that the terms "mutual fund" and "institutional investor" do not include an investor of a Contracting State which directly or indirectly owns 10 percent or more of the shares or other rights representing the capital or of the profits in a company that is a resident of the other Contracting State.

Finally, the State of residence of the alienator has the exclusive right to tax gains from the alienation of shares of a company that is a resident of the other Contracting State and whose shares are substantially and regularly traded on a recognized stock exchange located in that other State, provided that: (1) the shares were sold either on a recognized stock exchange in that other State or in a public offer for the acquisition of shares regulated by law; and (2) such shares were previously acquired either on a recognized stock exchange in that other State, in a public offer for the acquisition of such shares regulated by law, in a placement of first issue shares by that company at the time of the constitution of that company or of an increase in the capital of that company, or in an exchange of bonds convertible into shares.

Paragraph 7

Paragraph 7 sets forth two exceptions to the limitation imposed by paragraph 5 on the rate of source State tax. As stated in paragraph 4 of the 2010 Exchange of Notes, the provisions of paragraph 7 (and paragraph 5, discussed above) of Article 13 reflect the unique operation of Chile's integrated tax system and are intended to prevent the avoidance of the Additional Tax.

As provided in subparagraph 7(a), the State of source may tax gains derived by a resident of the other Contracting State if the recipient of the gain at any time during the 12-month period preceding the alienation owned shares, directly or indirectly, consisting of more than 50 percent of the capital of a company that is a resident of the first-mentioned State. As provided in subparagraph 7(b), the State of source may tax gains derived by a resident of the other Contracting State from the alienation of other rights not being shares or debt claims representing the capital of a company (such as a limited liability company) that is a resident of the first-mentioned State, if the recipient of the gain at any time during the 12-month period preceding the alienation owned other such rights, directly or indirectly, consisting of 20 percent or more of the capital of that company. Paragraph 16 of the Protocol provides that the rate of Additional Tax imposed by Chile under the provisions of paragraph 7 of Article 13 shall not exceed 35 percent.

Paragraph 16 of the Protocol provides that the rate of Additional Tax imposed by Chile under the provisions of paragraph 7 shall not exceed 35 percent. In addition, paragraph 16 of the Protocol provides that if under the domestic law of Chile, the First Category Tax exceeds 30 percent, paragraph 7 (and paragraph 5, discussed above) of Article 13 shall not apply. In such case, paragraph 4 of the 2010 Exchange of Notes provides that paragraph 16 of the Protocol will operate to limit the right of the source State to tax capital gains, and such gains will only be subject to tax in the residence State.

Under paragraph 22 of the Protocol, if Chile concludes with another state an income tax treaty that contains terms further limiting the right of the source State to tax capital gains under Article 13, the United States and Chile shall, at the request of the United States, consult to reassess the balance of benefits of the Convention with a view to concluding a protocol incorporating such lower rates into the Convention.

Paragraph 8

Paragraph 8 provides that the State of residence of the alienator has the exclusive right to tax gains from the alienation of any property other than property referred to in paragraphs 1 through 7.

Paragraph 9

The purpose of paragraph 9 is to provide a rule to address the mark-to-market exit tax regime for "covered expatriates" under Code section 877A. This rule is intended to coordinate United States and Chilean taxation of gains in the case of a timing mismatch. Such a mismatch may occur, for example, where a U.S. resident recognizes, for U.S. tax purposes, gain on a deemed sale of all property on the day before the individual expatriates to Chile. To avoid double taxation, paragraph 9 of Article 13 provides that where an individual who, upon ceasing to be a resident of one Contracting State, is treated for purposes of taxation by that State as having alienated a property and is taxed by that State by reason thereof, the individual may elect to be treated for the purposes of taxation by the other Contracting State as having sold and repurchased the property for its fair market value on the day before the expatriation date. The election in paragraph 9 therefore will be available to any individual who expatriates from the

United States to Chile. The effect of the election will be to give the individual an adjusted basis for Chilean tax purposes equal to the fair market value of the property as of the date of the deemed alienation in the United States, with the result that only post-emigration gain will be subject to Chilean tax when there is an actual alienation of the property while the individual is a resident of Chile.

If an individual recognizes in one Contracting State losses and gains from the deemed alienation of multiple properties, then the individual must apply paragraph 9 consistently with respect to all such properties. An individual who is deemed to have alienated multiple properties may only make the election under paragraph 9 if the deemed alienation of all such properties results in a net gain.

Paragraph 9 provides that an individual who ceases to be a resident of one of the Contracting States may not make the election with respect to property situated in the other Contracting State. In addition, an individual may make the election only with respect to property that is treated as sold for its fair market value under a Contracting State's deemed disposition rules. At the time the Convention was signed, the following were the types of property that were generally excluded from the deemed disposition rules in the case of individuals who cease to be citizens or long term residents of the United States: (1) an eligible deferred compensation item as defined under Code section 877A(d)(3); (2) a specified tax deferred account as defined under Code section 877A(e)(2); and (3) an interest in a non-grantor trust as defined under Code section 877A(f)(3).

Relationship to Other Articles

Notwithstanding the foregoing limitations on taxation of certain gains by the State of source, the saving clause of paragraph 4 of the Protocol permits the United States to tax its citizens and residents as if the Convention had not come into effect. Thus, any limitation in this Article on the right of the United States to tax gains does not apply to gains of a U.S. citizen or resident.

The benefits of this Article are also subject to the provisions of Article 24 (Limitation on Benefits). Thus, only a resident of a Contracting State that satisfies one of the conditions in Article 24 is entitled to the benefits of this Article.

ARTICLE 14 (INDEPENDENT PERSONAL SERVICES)

The Convention addresses in separate Articles the taxation of different classes of income from personal services. Article 14 concerns income from independent personal services, and Article 15 concerns income from dependent personal services. The Convention provides exceptions and additional rules for directors' fees (Article 16); income of artists and athletes (Article 17); pensions, social security benefits, alimony, and child support payments (Article 18); government service salaries (Article 19); and certain income of students and trainees (Article 20).

Paragraph 1

Paragraph 1 of Article 14 provides the general rule that an individual resident of a Contracting State who derives income from performing professional services in an independent capacity will not be taxed with respect to that income by the other Contracting State. Such income may also be taxed in the other Contracting State only if one of two tests is met. First, if a resident of a Contracting State has a fixed base regularly available to him in the host State for the purpose of performing his activities, the host State may tax only so much of the income that is attributable to that fixed base and is derived from services performed in any state other than the residence State. Second, if a resident of a Contracting State is present in the host State for a period or periods equaling or exceeding 183 days in any 12-month period that begins or ends during the relevant taxable year (*i.e.*, in the United States, the calendar year in which the services are performed), the host State may tax only so much of the income that is derived from the activities performed in the host State.

Paragraph 5 of the 2010 Exchange of Notes provides that "performed in that other State" does not mean "received in that other State." This clarifies that Article 14 does not apply, for example, to payments to a U.S. individual by a client in Chile for services that were performed in the United States.

Income derived by persons other than individuals or groups of individuals from the performance of independent personal services is not covered by Article 14. Such income generally would be business profits taxable in accordance with Article 7 (Business Profits). Income derived by employees of such persons generally would be taxable in accordance with Article 15 (Dependent Personal Services).

The term "fixed base" is not defined in the Convention, but its meaning is understood to be identical to that of the term "permanent establishment," as defined in Article 5 (Permanent Establishment). The term "regularly available" also is not defined in the Convention. Whether a fixed base is regularly available to a person will be determined based on all the facts and circumstances.

The 183-day period referred to in subparagraph 1(b) is to be measured using the "days of physical presence" method. Under this method, the days that are counted include any day in which a part of the day is spent in the host State. *See* Rev. Rul. 56-24, 1956-1 C.B. 851. Thus, days that are counted include the days of arrival and departure; weekends and holidays on which the employee does not work but is present within the State; vacation days spent in the host State before, during or after the employment period, unless the individual's presence before or after the employment can be shown to be independent of his presence there for employment purposes; and time during periods of sickness, training periods, strikes, etc., when the individual is present but not working. If illness prevented the individual from leaving the host State in sufficient time to qualify for the benefit, those days will not count. Also, any part of a day spent in the host State while in transit between two points outside the host State is not counted. If the individual is a resident of the host State for part of the taxable year concerned and a nonresident for the remainder of the year, the individual's days of presence as a resident do not count for purposes of determining whether the 183-day period is exceeded.

Paragraph 7 of Article 7 (Business Profits) clarifies that income that is attributable to a permanent establishment or fixed base but that is deferred and received after such permanent establishment or fixed base has ceased to exist may nevertheless be taxed by the State in which the permanent establishment or fixed base was located. Thus, under Article 14, income derived by an individual resident of a Contracting State from services performed in the other Contracting State and attributable to a fixed base there may be taxed by that other State even if the income is deferred and received after there is no longer a fixed base available to the resident in that other State.

Paragraph 2

Paragraph 2 provides that in cases where the host State may tax income from independent personal services under paragraph 1, the host State will do so only on a net basis, as if such income were attributable to a permanent establishment and taxable by the host State under Article 7. For purposes of paragraph 1, the principles of paragraph 3 of Article 7 (Business Profits) will apply to determine the income that is taxable in the host State, provided that related administrative requirements have been satisfied. Thus, all necessary expenses, including expenses not incurred in the host State, must be allowed as deductions in computing the net income from services subject to tax in the host State.

Paragraph 3

Paragraph 3 contains a non-exhaustive list of activities that constitute "professional services." The term includes independent scientific, literary, artistic, educational or teaching activities, as well as the independent activities of physicians, lawyers, engineers, architects, dentists, and accountants.

In addition to applying to income in respect of professional services, Article 14 also applies to income in respect of other activities of an independent character. This includes personal services performed by an individual for his own account, whether as a sole proprietor or a partner, where he receives the income and bears the risk of loss arising from the services. However, the taxation of income of an individual from those types of independent services which are covered by Articles 16 through 18 is governed by the provisions of those articles. For example, taxation of the income of a corporate director would be governed by Article 16 rather than Article 14.

This Article applies to income derived by a partner resident in the Contracting State that is attributable to personal services of an independent character performed in the other State through a partnership that has a fixed base in that other Contracting State. Income which may be taxed under this Article includes all income attributable to the fixed base in respect of the performance of the personal services carried on by the partnership (whether by the partner himself, other partners in the partnership, or by employees assisting the partners) and any income from activities ancillary to the performance of those services (for example, charges for facsimile services). Income that is not derived from the performance of personal services and that is not ancillary thereto (for example, rental income from subletting office space), will be governed by other Articles of the Convention.

The application of Article 14 to a service partnership may be illustrated by the following example: a partnership formed in a Contracting State has five partners (who agree to split profits equally), four of whom are resident and perform personal services only in that Contracting State at Office A, and one of whom performs personal services from Office B, a fixed base in the other Contracting State. In this case, the four partners of the partnership resident in the first-mentioned Contracting State may be taxed in the other Contracting State in respect of their share of the income attributable to the fixed base, Office B. The services giving rise to income which may be attributed to the fixed base would include not only the services performed by the one resident partner, but also, for example, if one of the four other partners came to the other Contracting State and worked on an Office B matter there, the income in respect of those services also. As noted above, this would be the case regardless of whether such partner from the first-mentioned Contracting State actually visited or used Office B when performing services in the other State.

Relationship to other Articles

This Article is subject to the provisions of the saving clause of paragraph 4 of the Protocol. Thus, if a resident of Chile who is a U.S. citizen performs independent personal services in the United States, the United States may tax his income without regard to the provisions of this Article, subject to the special foreign tax credit provisions of paragraph 3 of Article 23 (Relief from Double Taxation). In addition, as with other benefits of the Convention, the benefits of this Article are available to a resident of a Contracting State only if that resident is entitled to those benefits under Article 24 (Limitation on Benefits).

ARTICLE 15 (DEPENDENT PERSONAL SERVICES)

Article 15 apportions taxing jurisdiction over remuneration derived by a resident of a Contracting State as an employee between the States of source and residence.

Paragraph 1

The general rule of Article 15 is contained in paragraph 1. Remuneration derived by a resident of a Contracting State as an employee may be taxed by the State of residence, and the remuneration also may be taxed by the other Contracting State to the extent derived from employment exercised (*i.e.*, services performed) in that other Contracting State. Paragraph 1 also provides that the more specific rules of Articles 16 (Directors' Fees), 18 (Pensions, Social Security, Alimony and Child Support), and 19 (Government Service) apply in the case of employment income described in one of those articles. Thus, even though the State of source has a right to tax employment income under Article 15, it may not have the right to tax that income under the Convention if the income is described, for example, in Article 18 and is not taxable in the State of source under the provisions of that article.

Article 15 applies to any form of compensation for employment, including payments in kind. Paragraph 1.1 of the Commentary to Article 16 of the OECD Model is consistent with that interpretation.

Consistent with Code section 864(c)(6), Article 15 also applies regardless of the timing of actual payment for services. Consequently, a person who receives the right to a future payment in consideration for services rendered in a Contracting State would be taxable in that State even if the payment is received at a time when the recipient is a resident of the other Contracting State. Thus, a bonus paid to a resident of a Contracting State with respect to services performed in the other Contracting State with respect to a particular taxable year would be subject to Article 15 for that year even if it was paid after the close of the year. An annuity received for services performed in a taxable year could be subject to Article 15 despite the fact that it was paid in subsequent years. In that case, it would be necessary to determine whether the payment constitutes deferred compensation, taxable under Article 15, or a qualified pension subject to the rules of Article 18. Article 15 also applies to income derived from the exercise of stock options granted with respect to services performed in the host State, even if those stock options are exercised after the employee has left the host State. If Article 15 is found to apply, whether such payments were taxable in the State where the employment was exercised would depend on whether the requirements of paragraph 2 were satisfied in the year in which the services to which the payment relates were performed.

Paragraph 2

Paragraph 2 sets forth an exception to the general rule that employment income may be taxed in the State where it is exercised. Under paragraph 2, the State where the employment is exercised may not tax the income from the employment if three conditions are satisfied: (a) the individual is present in the other Contracting State for a period or periods not exceeding 183 days in any 12-month period that begins or ends during the relevant taxable year (*i.e.*, in the United States, the calendar year in which the services are performed); (b) the remuneration is paid by, or on behalf of, an employer who is not a resident of that other Contracting State; and (c) the remuneration is not borne as a deductible expense by a permanent establishment or a fixed base which the employer has in that other State. In order for the remuneration to be exempt from tax in the source State, all three conditions must be satisfied. This exception is identical to that set forth in the OECD Model.

The 183-day period in condition (a) is to be measured using the "days of physical presence" method. Under this method, the days that are counted include any day in which a part of the day is spent in the host State. *See* Rev. Rul. 56-24, 1956-1 C.B. 851. Thus, days that are counted include the days of arrival and departure; weekends and holidays on which the employee does not work but is present within the State; vacation days spent in the host State before, during or after the employment period, unless the individual's presence before or after the employment can be shown to be independent of his presence there for employment purposes; and time during periods of sickness, training periods, strikes, etc., when the individual is present but not working. If illness prevented the individual from leaving the host State in sufficient time to qualify for the benefit, those days will not count. Also, any part of a day spent in the host State while in transit between two points outside the host State is not counted. If the individual is a resident of the host State for part of the taxable year concerned and a nonresident for the remainder of the year, the individual's days of presence as a resident do not count for purposes of determining whether the 183-day period is exceeded.

Conditions (b) and (c) are intended to ensure that a Contracting State will not be required to allow a deduction to the payor for compensation paid and at the same time to exempt the employee on the amount received. Accordingly, if a foreign person pays the salary of an employee who is employed in the host State, but a host State corporation or permanent establishment reimburses the payor with a payment that can be identified as a reimbursement, neither condition (b) nor (c), as the case may be, will be considered to have been fulfilled.

The reference to remuneration "borne by" a permanent establishment is understood to encompass all expenses that economically are incurred and not merely expenses that are currently deductible for tax purposes. Accordingly, the expenses referred to include expenses that are capitalizable as well as those that are currently deductible. Further, salaries paid by residents that are exempt from income taxation may be considered to be borne by a permanent establishment notwithstanding the fact that the expenses will be neither deductible nor capitalizable since the payor is exempt from tax.

Paragraph 3

Paragraph 3 contains a special rule applicable to remuneration derived by a resident of a Contracting State as an employee aboard a ship or aircraft operated in international traffic. Such remuneration may be taxed only in the State of residence of the employee if the services are performed as a member of the regular complement of the ship or aircraft. The "regular complement" includes the crew. In the case of a cruise ship, for example, it may also include others, such as entertainers, lecturers, etc., employed by the shipping company to serve on the ship throughout its voyage. The use of the term "regular complement" is intended to clarify that a person who exercises his employment as, for example, an insurance salesman while aboard a ship or aircraft is not covered by this paragraph.

Relationship to other Articles

If a U.S. citizen who is resident in Chile performs services as an employee in the United States and meets the conditions of paragraph 2 for source State exemption, he nevertheless is taxable in the United States by virtue of the saving clause of paragraph 4 of the Protocol, subject to the special foreign tax credit rule of paragraph 3 of Article 23 (Relief from Double Taxation).

ARTICLE 16 (DIRECTORS' FEES)

This Article provides that directors' fees and other similar payments derived by a resident of a Contracting State in his capacity as a member of the board of directors or an equivalent body of a company that is a resident of the other Contracting State may be taxed by the State where such fees or payments arise. Such fees or payments will be deemed to arise in the State in which the company is resident, except to the extent that such fees or payments are paid in respect of attendance at meetings held in the other Contracting State.

This rule is an exception to the more general rules of Articles 7 (Business Profits), 14 (Independent Personal Services), and 15 (Dependent Personal Services). Thus, for example, in determining whether a director's fee paid to a non-employee director is subject to tax in the State of residence of the corporation, it is not relevant to establish whether the fee is attributable to a permanent establishment in that State.

ARTICLE 17 (ARTISTES AND SPORTSMEN)

This Article deals with the taxation in a Contracting State of entertainers and sportsmen resident in the other Contracting State from the performance of their services as such. The Article applies both to the income of an entertainer or sportsman who performs services on his own behalf and one who performs services on behalf of another person, either as an employee of that person, or pursuant to any other arrangement. The rules of this Article take precedence, in some circumstances, over those of Articles 14 (Independent Personal Services) and 15 (Dependent Personal Services).

This Article applies only with respect to the income of entertainers and sportsmen. Others involved in a performance or athletic event, such as producers, directors, technicians, managers, coaches, etc., remain subject to the provisions of Articles 14 and 15. In addition, except as provided in paragraph 2, income earned by juridical persons is not covered by Article 17.

Paragraph 1

Paragraph 1 describes the circumstances in which a Contracting State may tax the performance income of an entertainer or sportsman who is a resident of the other Contracting State. Under this paragraph, income derived by an individual resident of a Contracting State from activities as an entertainer or sportsman exercised in the other Contracting State may be taxed in that other State if the amount of the gross receipts derived by the performer equals or exceeds $5,000 (or its equivalent in Chilean pesos) for the taxable year. The $5,000 threshold includes expenses reimbursed to the individual or borne on his behalf. If the gross receipts exceed $5,000, the full amount, not just the excess, may be taxed in the State of performance.

The Convention introduces this monetary threshold to distinguish between two groups of entertainers and athletes – those who are paid relatively large sums of money for very short periods of service, and who would, therefore, normally be exempt from tax in the host State

57

under the standard personal services income rules, from those who earn relatively modest amounts and are, therefore, not easily distinguishable from those who earn other types of personal services income.

Tax may be imposed under paragraph 1 even if the performer would have been exempt from tax under Article 14 or 15. On the other hand, if the performer would be exempt from host-State tax under Article 17, but would be taxable under either Article 14 or 15, tax may be imposed under either of those Articles. Thus, for example, if a performer derives remuneration from his activities in an independent capacity, and the performer does not have a permanent establishment in the host State, he may be taxed by the host State in accordance with Article 17 if his remuneration equals or exceeds $5,000 annually, despite the fact that he generally would be exempt from host State taxation under Article 14 or 15. However, a performer who receives less than the $5,000 threshold amount and therefore is not taxable under Article 17 nevertheless may be subject to tax in the host State under Article 14 or 15 if the tests for host-State taxability under the relevant Article are met. For example, if an entertainer who is an independent contractor earns $14,000 of income in a State for the calendar year, but the income is attributable to his fixed base in the host State, that State may tax his income under Article 14 or 15.

As explained in paragraph 9 of the Commentary to Article 17 of the OECD Model, Article 17 of the Convention applies to all income connected with a performance by the entertainer, such as appearance fees, award or prize money, and a share of the gate receipts. Income derived from a Contracting State by a performer who is a resident of the other Contracting State from other than actual performance, such as royalties from record sales and payments for product endorsements, is not covered by this Article, but by other articles of the Convention, such as Article 12 (Royalties) or Article 7 (Business Profits). For example, if an entertainer receives royalty income from the sale of live recordings, the royalty income would be subject to the provisions of Article 12, even if the performance was conducted in the source State, although the entertainer could be taxed in the source State with respect to income from the performance itself under Article 17 if the $5,000 threshold is met.

In determining whether income falls under Article 17 or another article, the controlling factor will be whether the income in question is predominantly attributable to the performance itself or to other activities or property rights. For instance, a fee paid to a performer for endorsement of a performance in which the performer will participate would be considered to be so closely associated with the performance itself that it normally would fall within Article 17. Similarly, a sponsorship fee paid by a business in return for the right to attach its name to the performance would be so closely associated with the performance that it would fall under Article 17 as well. As indicated in paragraph 9 of the Commentary to Article 17 of the OECD Model, however, a cancellation fee would not be considered to fall within Article 17 but would be dealt with under Article 14 or 15.

As indicated in paragraph 4 of the Commentary to Article 17 of the OECD Model, where an individual fulfills a dual role as performer and non-performer (such as a player-coach or an actor-director), but his role in one of the two capacities is negligible, the predominant character of the individual's activities should control the characterization of those activities. In other cases there should be an apportionment between the performance-related compensation and other compensation.

Consistent with Articles 14 and 15, Article 17 also applies regardless of the timing of actual payment for services. Thus, a bonus paid to a resident of a Contracting State with respect to a performance in the other Contracting State during a particular taxable year would be subject to Article 17 for that year even if it was paid after the close of the year. The determination as to whether the $5,000 threshold has been met is determined separately with respect to each year of payment. Accordingly, if an actor who is a resident of one Contracting State receives residual payments over time with respect to a movie that was filmed in the other Contracting State, the payments do not have to be aggregated from one year to another to determine whether the total payments have finally equaled or exceeded $5,000. Otherwise, residual payments received many years later could retroactively subject all earlier payments to tax by the other Contracting State.

Paragraph 2

Paragraph 2 is intended to address the potential for circumvention of the rule in paragraph 1 when a performer's income does not accrue directly to the performer himself, but to another person. Foreign performers frequently perform in the United States as employees of, or under contract with, a company or other person.

The relationship may truly be one of employee and employer, with no circumvention of paragraph 1 either intended or realized. On the other hand, the "employer" may, for example, be a company established and owned by the performer, which is merely acting as the nominal income recipient in respect of the remuneration for the performance (a "star company"). The performer may act as an "employee," receive a modest salary, and arrange to receive the remainder of the income from his performance from the company in another form or at a later time. In such case, absent the provisions of paragraph 2, the income arguably could escape host-State tax because the company earns business profits but has no permanent establishment in that country. The performer may largely or entirely escape host-State tax by receiving only a small salary, perhaps small enough to place him below the dollar threshold in paragraph 1. The performer might arrange to receive further payments in a later year, when he is not subject to host-State tax, perhaps as dividends or liquidating distributions.

Paragraph 2 seeks to prevent this type of abuse while at the same time protecting the taxpayers' rights to the benefits of the Convention when there is a legitimate employee-employer relationship between the performer and the person providing his services. Under paragraph 2, when the income accrues to a person other than the performer, and the performer or any related persons participate, directly or indirectly, in the receipts or profits of that other person, the income may be taxed in the Contracting State where the performer's services are exercised, without regard to the provisions of the Convention concerning business profits (Article 7) or independent personal services income (Article 14).

In cases where paragraph 2 is applicable, the income of the "employer" may be subject to tax in the host State even if it has no permanent establishment or fixed base in the host State.

Taxation under paragraph 2 is on the person providing the services of the performer. This paragraph does not affect the rules of paragraph 1, which apply to the performer himself. The income taxable by virtue of paragraph 2 is reduced to the extent of salary payments to the performer, which fall under paragraph 1.

For purposes of paragraph 2, income is deemed to accrue to another person (*i.e.*, the person providing the services of the performer) if that other person has control over, or the right to receive, gross income in respect of the services of the performer. Direct or indirect participation in the profits of a person may include, but is not limited to, the accrual or receipt of deferred remuneration, bonuses, fees, dividends, partnership income or other distributions.

Paragraph 2 does not apply if it is established that neither the performer nor any persons related to the performer participate directly or indirectly in the receipts or profits of the person providing the services of the performer. Assume, for example, that a circus owned by a U.S. corporation performs in the other Contracting State, and promoters of the performance in the other State pay the circus, which, in turn, pays salaries to the circus performers. The circus is determined to have no permanent establishment in that State. Since the circus performers do not participate in the profits of the circus, but merely receive their salaries out of the circus' gross receipts, the circus is protected by Article 7 and its income is not subject to host-country tax. Whether the salaries of the circus performers are subject to host-country tax under this Article depends on whether they exceed the $5,000 threshold in paragraph 1.

Pursuant to Article 1 (General Scope) the Convention only applies to persons who are residents of one of the Contracting States. Thus, income of a star company that is not a resident of one of the Contracting States would not be eligible for benefits of the Convention.

Relationship to other Articles

This Article is subject to the provisions of the saving clause of paragraph 4 of the Protocol. Thus, if an entertainer or a sportsman who is resident of Chile is a citizen of the United States, the United States may tax all of his income from performances in the United States without regard to the provisions of this Article (subject to the special foreign tax credit provisions of paragraph 3 of Article 23 (Relief from Double Taxation)). In addition, benefits of this Article are subject to the provisions of Article 24 (Limitation on Benefits).

ARTICLE 18 (PENSIONS, SOCIAL SECURITY, ALIMONY AND CHILD SUPPORT)

This Article deals with the taxation of pension payments (both private and government), social security benefits, contributions to pension funds, and alimony and child support payments.

Paragraph 1

Paragraph 1 deals with the taxation of private (*i.e.*, non-government service) pension payments and other similar remuneration in consideration of past employment that are derived from sources within one Contracting State and beneficially owned by a resident of the other

Contracting State. The term "pension payments and other similar remuneration" includes both periodic and single sum payments. The taxation of annuity payments that are not in consideration of past employment is dealt with in Article 21 (Other Income) of the Convention.

Subparagraph 1(a) provides that pension payments and other similar remuneration that are derived from sources within one Contracting State and beneficially owned by a resident of the other Contracting State are taxable in both Contracting States. However, the tax imposed by the source State may not exceed 15 percent of the gross amount of such payment.

Subparagraph 1(b) contains an exception to the State of residence's right to tax pension payments and other similar remuneration under subparagraph 1(a). Under subparagraph 1(b), the State of residence must exempt from tax any amount of such payment that would be exempt from tax in the Contracting State in which the pension plan is established if the recipient were a resident of that State. Thus, for example, a distribution from certain individual retirement accounts ("IRAs"), such as a U.S. "Roth IRA" to a resident of Chile would be exempt from tax in Chile to the same extent the distribution would be exempt from tax in the United States if it were distributed to a U.S. resident. The same is true with respect to distributions from a traditional IRA to the extent that the distribution represents a return of non-deductible contributions. Similarly, if distributions from a traditional IRA were not subject to U.S. tax because they were "rolled over" to another U.S. IRA, then the distributions would be exempt from tax in Chile.

Paragraph 1 is intended to cover payments made by qualified private retirement plans. In the United States, the plans covered by paragraph 1 include qualified plans under Code section 401(a), individual retirement plans (including individual retirement plans that are part of a simplified employee pension plan that satisfies Code section 408(k), individual retirement accounts, and Code section 408(p) accounts), Code section 403(a) qualified annuity plans, and Code section 403(b) plans. Distributions from Code section 457 plans may also fall under paragraph 1 if they are not paid with respect to government services. The competent authorities may agree that distributions from other plans that generally meet criteria similar to those applicable to the listed plans also qualify for the benefits of paragraph 1. Payments in consideration of past employment in the private sector that are not eligible for the benefits of paragraph 1 generally are covered by Article 15 (Dependent Personal Services).

Pensions in respect of government service and social security benefits are not covered by paragraph 1. Pensions in respect of government service are generally covered by paragraph 2, while social security benefits are covered by paragraph 3.

Paragraph 2

Paragraph 2 deals with the taxation of pensions paid from the public funds of a Contracting State, or a political subdivision or a local authority thereof, to an individual in respect of services rendered to that State or subdivision or authority. Subparagraph 2(a) provides that such pensions are taxable only in that State. Subparagraph 2(b) provides an exception under which such pensions are taxable only in the other State if the individual is a resident of, and a national of, that other State.

Pensions paid to retired civilian and military employees of a Government of either State are intended to be covered under paragraph 2. When benefits paid by a State in respect of services rendered to that State or a subdivision or local authority are in the form of social security benefits, however, those payments are covered by paragraph 3. As a general matter, the result will be the same whether paragraph 2 or 3 applies, since both pensions in respect of government service and social security benefits are taxable exclusively by the source State. The result will differ only when the payment is made to a national and resident of the other Contracting State, who is not also a citizen of the paying State (or, where the United States is the paying State, a lawful permanent resident of the United States). In such a case, social security benefits continue to be taxable at source while government pensions become taxable only in the residence State.

In the case of the United States, paragraph 2 generally covers payments from Code section 457(g), 401(a), 403(a), and 403(b) plans established for U.S. government employees, as well as payments from the Thrift Savings Fund (Code section 7701(j)).

Paragraph 3

Paragraph 3 deals with the taxation of social security benefits. This paragraph provides that, notwithstanding the provisions of paragraphs 1 and 2, payments made by one of the Contracting States under the provisions of its social security or similar legislation to a resident of the other Contracting State or to a citizen of the United States will be taxable only in the Contracting State making the payment. The reference to U.S. citizens is necessary to ensure that a social security payment by Chile to a U.S. citizen who is not resident in the United States will not be taxable by the United States.

Paragraph 3 applies to social security benefits, regardless of whether the beneficiary contributed to the system as a private sector or Government employee. Payments made under provisions of the social security or similar legislation of a Contracting State include payments made pursuant to a pension plan or fund created under the social security system of that State. Paragraph 18 of the Protocol provides that in the case of Chile, the social security system referred to in paragraph 3 of Article 18 is any pension scheme or fund administered by the *Instituto de Prevision Social* (formerly *Instituto de Normalización Previsional*) and the social security system created by Decree Law 3500 (*DL 3500*). In the case of the United States, the phrase "similar legislation" is intended to refer to U.S. Tier 1 Railroad Retirement benefits.

Paragraph 4

Paragraph 4 provides that, if a resident of a Contracting State is a beneficiary of a pension plan established in the other Contracting State that is generally exempt from income taxation in that other State and operated to provide pension or retirement benefits, neither State will tax the income earned but not distributed by the plan until a payment or other similar remuneration is made from the plan. Thus, for example, if a U.S. citizen contributes to a U.S. qualified plan while working in the United States and then establishes residence in Chile, this paragraph ensures that neither the United States nor Chile will tax currently the plan's earnings and accretions with respect to that individual. Only at the time and to the extent that a payment or other similar remuneration is made from the plan (and not transferred to another pension fund in the United States), may the payment be subject to tax subject to the provisions of paragraph 1 of Article 18. Thus, if a distribution from a pension plan established in a Contracting State is not currently taxable in that State because it is rolled over into another pension plan in that State, such distribution shall also not be subject to tax in the other Contracting State.

Paragraph 5

Paragraph 5 provides certain benefits with respect to contributions to a pension fund in the case of a short-term assignment where an individual participates in a pension fund in one State (the "home State") and performs services (whether or not as an employee) for a limited period of time in the other State (the "host State"). It is not necessary for an individual to be a resident of the host State in order to claim the benefits of paragraph 5 (as long as the individual does not become a citizen or permanent resident of the host State). However, benefits are available under paragraph 5 only for so long as the individual performs services in a period not exceeding an aggregate of 60 months.

If the requirements of paragraph 5 are satisfied, contributions paid by, or on behalf of, the individual with respect to the services performed in the host State to a pension fund that is generally exempt from income tax in the home State and operated primarily to provide pension or retirement benefits in the home State (whether or not sponsored by an employer) will be treated in the same way for tax purposes in the host State as a contribution paid to a pension plan that is generally exempt from income tax in the host State and operated primarily to provide pension or retirement benefits in the host State. Thus, for example, if a participant in a U.S. qualified plan goes to work temporarily in Chile, contributions to the U.S. qualified plan will be treated for tax purposes in Chile as contributions to a pension plan that is generally exempt in Chile and operated primarily to provide pension or retirement benefits in Chile.

Under subparagraph 5(a), the individual must have been already contributing on a regular basis to the pension plan, or to another similar plan for which the first-mentioned plan was substituted, for a period ending immediately before the individual became a resident or is temporarily present in the host State. The rule regarding substituted plans would be satisfied, for example, if the employer has been acquired by a company that replaces the existing plan with its own plan, transferring membership in the old plan over into the new plan.

Under subparagraph 5(b), the competent authority of the host State must determine that the home State plan to which the contribution is made generally corresponds to a pension plan recognized for tax purposes by the host State. For this purpose, paragraph 19 of the Protocol provides that the Chilean pension plans eligible for the benefits of paragraph 5 of Article 18 include the following and any identical or substantially similar plan that is established pursuant to legislation introduced after the date of signature of the Protocol: any pension scheme or fund

63

administered by the *Instituto de Prevision Social* (formerly *Instituto de Normalización Previsional*) and the social security system created by Decree Law 3500 (*DL 3500*).

Paragraph 19 of the Protocol also provides that the U.S. plans eligible for the benefits of paragraph 5 of Article 18 include the following and any identical or substantially similar plan that is established pursuant to legislation introduced after the date of signature of the Protocol: qualified plans under Code section 401(a) (including Code section 401(k) arrangements), individual retirement plans (including individual retirement plans that are part of a simplified employee pension plan that satisfies section 408(k), individual retirement accounts, and Code section 408(p) simple retirement accounts), Code section 403(a) qualified annuity plans, Code section 403(b) plans, Code section 457(g) trusts providing benefits under Code section 457(b) plans, and the Thrift Savings Fund (Code section 7701(j)).

If a particular plan in one Contracting State is of a type specified in paragraph 19 of the Protocol, it will not be necessary for taxpayers to obtain a determination from the competent authority of the other Contracting State that the plan generally corresponds to a pension or retirement plan established in and recognized for tax purposes in that State. A taxpayer who believes a particular plan in one Contracting State that is not described in paragraph 19 of the Protocol nevertheless satisfies the requirement of paragraph 5 of Article 18 may request a determination from the competent authority of the other Contracting State that the plan generally corresponds to a pension plan recognized for tax purposes by that State. In the case of the United States, such a determination must be requested under Revenue Procedure 2006-54, 2006-2 C.B. 1035 (or any applicable analogous or successor guidance).

Paragraph 5 applies only to the extent of the relief allowed by the host State to residents of that State for contributions to, or benefits accrued under, a pension plan established in the host State. Therefore, where the United States is the host State, the amount of contributions that may be excluded from an employee's income under this paragraph for U.S. tax purposes is limited to the U.S. dollar amount specified in Code section 415 or the U.S. dollar amount specified in section 402(g) to the extent contributions are made from the employee's compensation. For this purpose, the dollar limit specified in section 402(g)(1) means the amount applicable under section 402(g)(1) (including the age 50 catch-up amount in section 402(g)(1)(C)) or, if applicable, the parallel dollar limit applicable under section 457(e)(15) plus the age 50 catch-up amount under section 414(v)(2)(B)(i) for a section 457(g) trust.

Paragraph 5 does not address the treatment of employer contributions.

Paragraph 6

Paragraph 6 deals with alimony and child support payments. Periodic payments made pursuant to a written separation agreement or a decree of divorce, separate maintenance or compulsory support, including payments for the support of a child, paid by a resident of a Contracting State to a resident of the other Contracting State generally are taxable in neither Contracting State. However, if the payer is entitled to relief from tax for such payments in the first-mentioned State, such payments will be taxable only in the other State.

Relationship to other Articles

Under subparagraph 4(a) of the Protocol, paragraphs 1(b), 3, 4 and 6 of Article 18 are excepted from the saving clause of paragraph 4 of the Protocol. Thus, the United States will not tax U.S. citizens and residents on the income described in those paragraphs even if such amounts otherwise would be subject to tax under U.S. law.

Under subparagraph 4(b) of the Protocol, paragraphs 2 and 5 of Article 18 are excepted from the saving clause but only with respect to individuals who are neither citizens of the Contracting State conferring the benefits nor persons who have been admitted for permanent residence in that State (*i.e.*, in the United States, "green card" holders). Accordingly, for example, pension payments from the public funds of Chile to a U.S. permanent resident or citizen who is a Chilean national and resident (under paragraph 2 of Article 4) may be taxed by the United States pursuant to paragraph 4 of the Protocol even though such payments would be taxable only by Chile under paragraph 2 of Article 18. Similarly, if the United States is the host State for purposes of paragraph 5 of Article 18, a person who becomes a U.S. permanent resident or citizen will not be entitled to a deduction or exclusion for contributions to a pension plan established in Chile notwithstanding the provisions of paragraph 5 of Article 18.

ARTICLE 19 (GOVERNMENT SERVICE)

Paragraph 1

Subparagraphs 1(a) and 1(b) deal with the taxation of government compensation other than pensions which are addressed by paragraph 2 of Article 18 (Pensions, Social Security, Alimony and Child Support). Subparagraph 1(a) provides that salaries, wages, and other remuneration, other than a pension, paid to any individual who rendered services to a Contracting State, political subdivision or local authority are taxable only in that State. Under subparagraph 1(b), such payments are, however, taxable exclusively in the other State (the host State) if the services are rendered in the host State and the individual is a resident of the host State who is either a national of that State or did not become a resident of that State solely for purposes of rendering the services. The paragraph applies to anyone performing services of a governmental nature for a government, whether as a government employee, an independent contractor, or an employee of an independent contractor.

Paragraph 2

Paragraph 2 provides that the remuneration described in paragraph 1 will be subject to the rules of Articles 15 (Dependent Personal Services), 16 (Directors' Fees), and 17 (Artistes and Sportsmen) if the services rendered by an individual are in connection with a business conducted by a government.

Relationship to other Articles

Under subparagraph 4(b) of the Protocol, the saving clause does not apply to the benefits conferred by one of the States under Article 19 if the recipient of the benefits is neither a citizen of that State nor a person who has been admitted for permanent residence there (*i.e.*, in the United States, a "green card" holder). Thus, a resident of the United States who in the course of performing functions of a governmental nature becomes a resident of Chile (but not a permanent resident), would be entitled to the benefits of this Article.

ARTICLE 20 (STUDENTS AND TRAINEES)

This Article provides rules for host-State taxation of visiting students, apprentices, and business trainees. Persons who meet the tests of the Article will be exempt from tax in the State that they are visiting with respect to designated classes of income. Several conditions must be satisfied in order for an individual to be entitled to the benefits of this Article.

First, the visitor must have been, either at the time of his arrival in the host State or immediately before, a resident of the other Contracting State.

Second, the purpose of the visit must be the full-time education at a recognized educational institution such as a university, college or school, or full-time training of the visitor. Thus, if the visitor comes principally to work in the host State but also is a part-time student, he would not be entitled to the benefits of this Article, even with respect to any payments he may receive from abroad for his maintenance, education or training, and regardless of whether or not he is in a degree program. Whether a student is to be considered full-time will be determined by the rules of the educational institution at which he is studying.

The host-State exemption applies to payments that are received by the student, apprentice or business trainee for the purposes of his maintenance, education or training and that arise or are remitted from outside the host State. A payment will be considered to arise outside the host State if the payer is located outside the host State. Thus, if an employer from one of the Contracting States sends an employee to the other Contracting State for full-time training, the payments the trainee receives from abroad from his employer for his maintenance or training while he is present in the host State will be exempt from tax in the host State. Where appropriate, substance prevails over form in determining the identity of the payer. Thus, for example, payments made directly or indirectly by a U.S. person with whom the visitor is training, but which have been routed through a source outside the United States (*e.g.*, a foreign subsidiary), are not treated as arising outside the United States for this purpose.

In the case of an apprentice or business trainee, the benefits of the Article will extend only for a period of not exceeding two years from the date the visitor first arrives in the host State for the purpose of training. If, however, a trainee remains in the host country for a third year, thus losing the benefits of the Article, he would not retroactively lose the benefits of the Article for the first two years.

Relationship to other Articles

The saving clause of paragraph 4 of the Protocol does not apply to this Article with respect to an individual who is neither a citizen of the host State nor has been admitted for permanent residence there. The saving clause, however, does apply with respect to citizens and permanent residents of the host State. Thus, a U.S. citizen who is a resident of Chile and who visits the United States as a full-time student at an accredited university will not be exempt from U.S. tax on remittances from abroad that otherwise constitute U.S. taxable income. A person, however, who is not a U.S. citizen, and who visits the United States as a student and remains long enough to become a resident under U.S. law, but does not become a permanent resident (*i.e.*, does not acquire a green card), will be entitled to the full benefits of the Article.

ARTICLE 21 (OTHER INCOME)

Article 21 assigns taxing jurisdiction over income not dealt with in the other Articles (Articles 6 through 20) of the Convention. In order for an item of income to be "dealt with" in another Article it must be the type of income described in the article and, in most cases, it must have its source in a Contracting State. For example, all royalty income that arises in a Contracting State and that is beneficially owned by a resident of the other Contracting State is "dealt with" in Article 12 (Royalties). However, profits derived in the conduct of a business are "dealt with" in Article 7 (Business Profits) whether or not they have their source in one of the Contracting States.

Examples of items of income covered by Article 21 include income from gambling, punitive (but not compensatory) damages and covenants not to compete. The article would also apply to income from a variety of financial transactions, where such income does not arise in the course of the conduct of a trade or business. For example, income from notional principal contracts and other derivatives would fall within Article 21 if derived by persons not engaged in the trade or business of dealing in such instruments, unless such instruments were being used to hedge risks arising in a trade or business. It would also apply to securities lending fees derived by an institutional investor. Further, in most cases guarantee fees paid within an intercompany group would be covered by Article 21, unless the guarantor were engaged in the business of providing such guarantees to unrelated parties.

Article 21 also applies to items of income that are not dealt with in the other articles because of their source or some other characteristic. For example, Article 11 (Interest) addresses only the taxation of interest arising in a Contracting State. Interest arising in a third State that is not attributable to a permanent establishment, therefore, is subject to Article 21.

Distributions from partnerships are not generally dealt with under Article 21 because partnership distributions generally do not constitute income. Under the Code, partners include in income their distributive share of partnership income annually, and partnership distributions themselves generally do not give rise to income. This would also be the case under U.S. law with respect to distributions from trusts. Trust income and distributions that, under the Code, have the character of the associated distributable net income would generally be covered by another article of the Convention. *See* Code section 641, et seq.

Paragraph 1

The general rule of Article 21 is contained in paragraph 1. Items of income not dealt with in other Articles that are earned by a resident of a Contracting State will be taxable only in the State of residence. This right of taxation applies whether or not the residence State exercises its right to tax the income covered by the Article. The residence taxation provided by paragraph 1 applies only when a resident of a Contracting State is the beneficial owner of the income. This is understood from the phrase "income of a resident of a Contracting State." Thus, source taxation of income not dealt with in other articles of the Convention is not limited by paragraph 1 if it is nominally paid to a resident of the other Contracting State, but is beneficially owned by a resident of a third State. In addition, as discussed in greater detail below, where income not dealt with in other Articles of the Convention arises in the other Contracting State, paragraphs 2 and 3 permit source-State taxation.

Paragraph 2

This paragraph provides an exception to the general rule of paragraph 1 for income, other than income from immovable property as defined in paragraph 2 of Article 6 (Income from Real Property (Immovable Property)), that is effectively connected to a permanent establishment or fixed base maintained in a Contracting State by a resident of the other Contracting State. The taxation of such income is governed by the provisions of Article 7 (Business Profits) or 14 (Independent Personal Services), as the case may be. Therefore, for example, income arising outside the United States that is attributable to a permanent establishment maintained in the United States by a resident of Chile generally would be taxable by the United States under the provisions of Article 7. This would be true even if the income is sourced in a third State.

Paragraph 3

Notwithstanding the provisions of paragraphs 1 and 2, income of a resident of one of the Contracting States not dealt with in other articles and arising in the other State may also be taxed in that other State.

Relationship to Other Articles

This Article is subject to the saving clause of paragraph 4 of the Protocol. Thus, the United States may tax the income of a resident of Chile that is not dealt with elsewhere in the Convention, if that resident is a citizen of the United States. The Article is also subject to the provisions of Article 24 (Limitation on Benefits).

ARTICLE 22 (CAPITAL)

This Article specifies the circumstances in which a Contracting State may impose tax on capital owned by a resident of the other Contracting State. At the time of the signing of the Convention, neither the United States nor Chile imposed taxes on capital. Nevertheless, the Article is drafted in a reciprocal manner. The Article was included at Chile's request.

The Article provides the general rule in paragraph 4 that capital owned by a resident of a Contracting State may be taxed only by that Contracting State. Thus, in general, the source State cannot tax a resident of the other State on capital owned by that resident. Exceptions to this general rule are provided in paragraphs 1 and 2.

Paragraphs 1 and 2

Paragraph 1 provides that capital represented by real property (immovable property) (as defined in Article 6 (Income from Real Property (Immovable Property)) which is owned by a resident of a Contracting State and located in the other State may be taxed by that other State. Under paragraph 2, the source State may tax capital which is represented by personal property (movable property) which is part of the business property of a permanent establishment maintained in that State by an enterprise of the other State or which pertains to a fixed base maintained in the source State by a resident of the other State.

Paragraph 3

Paragraph 3 deals with capital represented by ships, aircraft and containers owned by a resident of a Contracting State and operated in international traffic, and by personal property (movable property) pertaining to the operation of such ships, aircraft or containers. Under the paragraph, such capital is taxable only in the residence State. Thus, for example, capital represented by ships owned by a resident of the United States and operated in international traffic will be exempt from capital tax in Chile.

Paragraph 4

Paragraph 4 provides that all other elements of capital of a resident of a Contracting State shall be taxable only in that State.

ARTICLE 23 (RELIEF FROM DOUBLE TAXATION)

This Article describes the manner in which each Contracting State undertakes to relieve double taxation. The United States uses the foreign tax credit method under its domestic law, and by treaty.

Paragraph 1

The United States agrees, in paragraph 1, to allow to its citizens and residents a credit against U.S. tax for income taxes paid or accrued to Chile. For this purpose, paragraph 1 provides that the taxes referred to in subparagraph 3(b) and paragraph 4 of Article 2 (Taxes Covered), excluding taxes on capital, are considered income taxes.

Subparagraph 1(b) provides for a deemed-paid credit, consistent with Code section 902, to a U.S. corporation in respect of dividends received from a corporation resident in Chile of which the U.S. corporation owns at least 10 percent of the voting stock. This credit is for the tax paid by the corporation to Chile on the profits out of which the dividends are considered paid.

The credits allowed under paragraph 1 are allowed in accordance with the provisions and subject to the limitations of U.S. law, as that law may be amended over time, so long as the general principle of the Article, that is, the allowance of a credit, is retained. Thus, although the Convention provides for a foreign tax credit, the terms of the credit are generally determined by the U.S. domestic law in effect for the taxable year for which the credit is allowed. *See, e.g.,* Code sections 901-909 and the regulations under those sections. For example, a foreign levy is not a tax to the extent a person subject to the levy receives (or will receive), directly or indirectly, a specific economic benefit from the foreign country in exchange for payment pursuant to the levy. *See* Treas. Reg. § 1.901-2(a)(2). In addition, the credit generally is limited to the amount of U.S. tax due with respect to net foreign source income within the relevant foreign tax credit limitation category (*see* Code section 904(a) and (d)), and the dollar amount of the credit is determined in accordance with U.S. currency translation rules (*see, e.g.,* Code section 986). Similarly, U.S. law applies to determine carryover periods for excess credits and other inter-year adjustments.

Paragraph 2

Paragraph 2 provides that Chile will provide relief from double taxation through the credit method. Chile agrees in paragraph 2, in accordance with and subject to the provisions of the law of Chile, to allow a credit against Chilean tax for income taxes payable on income from sources outside Chile.

Paragraph 3

Paragraph 3 provides special rules for the tax treatment in both States of certain types of income derived from U.S. sources by U.S. citizens who are residents of Chile. Since U.S. citizens, regardless of residence, are subject to United States tax at ordinary progressive rates on their worldwide income, the U.S. tax on the U.S. source income of a U.S. citizen resident in Chile may exceed the U.S. tax that may be imposed under the Convention on an item of U.S. source income derived by a resident of Chile who is not a U.S. citizen. The provisions of paragraph 3 ensure that Chile does not bear the cost of U.S. taxation of its citizens who are residents of Chile.

Subparagraph 3(a) provides, with respect to items of income from sources within the United States, special credit rules for Chile. These rules apply to items of U.S.-source income that would be either exempt from U.S. tax or subject to reduced rates of U.S. tax under the provisions of the Convention if they had been received by a resident of Chile who is not a U.S. citizen. The tax credit allowed under paragraph 3 with respect to such items need not exceed the U.S. tax that may be imposed under the Convention, other than tax imposed solely by reason of the U.S. citizenship of the taxpayer under the provisions of the saving clause of paragraph 4 of the Protocol.

For example, if a U.S. citizen resident in Chile receives a payment of royalties described in subparagraph 3(b) of Article 12 (Royalties) from sources within the United States, the foreign tax credit granted by Chile would be limited to 10 percent of the gross amount of the royalties – the U.S. tax that may be imposed under subparagraph 2(b) of Article 12 – even if the shareholder is subject to U.S. net income tax because of his U.S. citizenship.

Subparagraph 3(b) of Article 23 eliminates the potential for double taxation that can arise because subparagraph 3(a) provides that Chile need not provide full relief for the U.S. tax imposed on its citizens resident in Chile. Subparagraph 3(b) provides that the United States will credit the income tax paid or accrued to Chile, after the application of subparagraph 3(a). It further provides that in allowing the credit, the United States will not reduce its tax below the amount that is taken into account in Chile in applying subparagraph 3(a).

Since the income described in subparagraph 3(a) generally will be U.S. source income, special rules are required to re-source some of the income to Chile in order for the United States to be able to credit the tax paid to Chile. This re-sourcing is provided for in subparagraph 3(c), which deems the items of income referred to in subparagraph 3(a) to be from foreign sources to the extent necessary to avoid double taxation under paragraph 3(b). Paragraph 3 of Article 26 (Mutual Agreement Procedure) provides a mechanism by which the competent authorities can resolve any disputes regarding whether income is from sources within the United States.

The following two examples illustrate the application of paragraph 3 in the case of U.S.-source royalties described in subparagraph 3(b) of Article 12 (Royalties) received by a U.S. citizen resident in Chile. In both examples, the U.S. rate of tax on residents of Chile, under subparagraph 2(b) of Article 12, is 10 percent. In both examples, the U.S. income tax rate on the U.S. citizen is 35 percent. In example 1, the rate of income tax imposed in Chile on its resident (the U.S. citizen) is 25 percent (below the U.S. rate), and in example 2, the rate imposed on its resident is 40 percent (above the U.S. rate).

	Example 1	Example 2
Subparagraph (a)		
U.S.-source royalty payment	$100.00	$100.00
Notional U.S. withholding tax (Article 12(2)(b))	10.00	10.00
Taxable income in Chile	100.00	100.00
Chilean tax before credit	25.00	40.00
Less: tax credit for notional U.S. withholding tax	10.00	10.00
Net post-credit tax paid to Chile	15.00	30.00
Subparagraphs (b) and (c)		
U.S. pre-tax income	$100.00	$100.00
U.S. pre-credit citizenship tax	35.00	35.00
Notional U.S. withholding tax	10.00	10.00
U.S. tax eligible to be offset by credit	25.00	25.00

Tax paid to Chile	15.00	30.00
Income re-sourced from U.S. to foreign source (see below)	42.86	71.43
U.S. pre-credit tax on re-sourced income	15.00	25.00
U.S. credit for tax paid to Chile	15.00	25.00
Net post-credit U.S. tax	10.00	0.00
Total U.S. tax	20.00	10.00

In both examples, in the application of subparagraph 3(a), Chile credits a 10 percent U.S. tax against its residence tax on the U.S. citizen. In the first example, the net tax paid to Chile after the foreign tax credit is $15.00; in the second example, it is $30.00. In the application of subparagraphs 3(b) and 3(c), from the U.S. tax due before credit of $35.00, the United States subtracts the amount of the U.S. source tax of $10.00, against which no U.S. foreign tax credit is allowed. This subtraction ensures that the United States collects the tax that it is due under the Convention as the State of source.

In both examples, given the 35 percent U.S. tax rate, the maximum amount of U.S. tax against which credit for the tax paid to Chile may be claimed is $25 ($35 U.S. tax minus $10 U.S. withholding tax). Initially, all of the income in both examples was from sources within the United States. For a U.S. foreign tax credit to be allowed for the full amount of the tax paid to Chile, an appropriate amount of the income must be treated as foreign-source income under subparagraph 3(c).

The amount that must be re-sourced depends on the amount of tax for which the U.S. citizen is claiming a U.S. foreign tax credit. In example 1, the tax paid to Chile was $15. For this amount to be creditable against U.S. tax, $42.86 ($15 tax divided by 35 percent U.S. tax rate) must be re-sourced as foreign-source income. When the tax is credited against the $15 of U.S. tax on this re-sourced income, there is a net U.S. tax of $10 due after credit ($25 U.S. tax eligible to be offset by credit, minus $15 tax paid to Chile). Thus, in example 1, there is a total of $20 in U.S. tax ($10 U.S. withholding tax plus $10 residual U.S. tax).

In example 2, the tax paid to Chile was $30, but, because the United States subtracts the U.S. withholding tax of $10 from the total U.S. tax of $35, only $25 of U.S. taxes may be offset by taxes paid to Chile. Accordingly, the amount that must be re-sourced to Chile is limited to the amount necessary to ensure a U.S. foreign tax credit for $25 of tax paid to Chile, or $71.43 ($25 tax paid to the other Contracting State divided by 35 percent U.S. tax rate). When the tax paid to Chile is credited against the U.S. tax on this re-sourced income, there is no residual U.S. tax ($25 U.S. tax minus $30 tax paid to Chile, subject to the U.S. limit of $25). Thus, in example 2, there is a total of $10 in U.S. tax ($10 U.S. withholding tax plus $0 residual U.S. tax). Because the tax paid to Chile was $30 and the U.S. tax eligible to be offset by credit was $25, there is $5 of excess foreign tax credit available for carryover.

Paragraph 4

Paragraph 4 provides that where in accordance with the Convention income derived or capital owned by a resident of a Contracting State is exempt from tax in that State, such State may nevertheless take into account the exempted income or capital in calculating the amount of tax on the remaining income or capital of such person. This rule provides for "exemption with progression."

Paragraph 5

Paragraph 5 provides that certain items of gross income that would be otherwise treated as from sources within a Contracting State will be treated as income from sources within the other Contracting State for the purposes of allowing relief of double taxation pursuant to Article 23. Paragraph 5 is intended to ensure that a resident of a Contracting State can obtain an appropriate amount of foreign tax credit for income taxes paid to the other Contracting State when the Convention assigns to such other State primary taxing rights over an item of gross income.

Accordingly, for example, if the Convention allows Chile to tax an item of gross income (as defined under U.S. law) derived by a resident of the United States, the United States will treat that item of gross income as gross income from sources within Chile for U.S. foreign tax credit purposes. In the case of a U.S.-owned foreign corporation, however, section 904(h)(10) may apply for purposes of determining the U.S. foreign tax credit with respect to income subject to this re-sourcing rule. Section 904(h)(10) generally applies the foreign tax credit limitation separately to re-sourced income. *See also* Code sections 865(h) and 904(d)(6). Because paragraph 5 applies to items of gross income, not net income, U.S. expense allocation and apportionment rules, *see, e.g.*, Treas. Reg. sections 1.861-9 and -9T, continue to apply to income re-sourced under paragraph 5.

Relationship to other Articles

Article 23 is not subject to the saving clause of paragraph 4 of the Protocol. Thus, the United States will allow a credit to its citizens and residents in accordance with the Article, even if such credit were to provide a benefit not available under the Code (such as the re-sourcing provided by subparagraph 3(c) and paragraph 5).

ARTICLE 24 (LIMITATION ON BENEFITS)

Article 24 contains anti-treaty-shopping provisions that are intended to prevent residents of third countries from benefiting from what is intended to be a reciprocal agreement between two countries. In general, the provision does not rely on a determination of purpose or intention but instead sets forth a series of objective tests. A resident of a Contracting State that satisfies one of the tests will receive benefits regardless of its motivations in choosing its particular business structure.

The structure of the Article is as follows: Paragraph 1 states the general rule that residents are entitled to benefits otherwise accorded to residents only to the extent provided in the Article. Paragraph 2 lists a series of attributes of a resident of a Contracting State, the presence of any one of which will entitle that person to all the benefits of the Convention. Paragraph 3 provides that, regardless of whether a person qualifies for benefits under paragraph 2, benefits may be granted to that person with regard to certain income earned in the conduct of an active trade or business. Paragraph 4 provides that benefits also may be granted if the competent authority of the State from which benefits are claimed determines that it is appropriate to provide benefits in that case. Paragraph 5 provides special rules for so-called "triangular cases" notwithstanding paragraphs 1 through 4 of the Article. Paragraph 6 defines certain terms used in the Article.

Paragraph 1

Paragraph 1 provides that, except as otherwise provided, a resident of a Contracting State will be entitled to the benefits otherwise accorded to residents of a Contracting State under the Convention only to the extent provided in the Article. The benefits otherwise accorded to residents under the Convention include all limitations on source-based taxation under Articles 6 through 22, the treaty-based relief from double taxation provided by Article 23 (Relief from Double Taxation), and the protection afforded to residents of a Contracting State under Article 25 (Non-Discrimination). Some provisions do not require that a person be a resident in order to enjoy the benefits of those provisions. Article 26 (Mutual Agreement Procedure) is not limited to residents of the Contracting States, and Article 28 (Members of Diplomatic Missions and Consular Posts) applies to diplomatic agents or consular officials regardless of residence. Article 24 accordingly does not limit the availability of treaty benefits under these provisions.

Article 24 and the anti-abuse provisions of domestic law complement each other, as Article 24 effectively determines whether an entity has a sufficient nexus to the Contracting State to be treated as a resident for treaty purposes, while domestic anti-abuse provisions (*e.g.*, business purpose, substance-over-form, step transaction or conduit principles) determine whether a particular transaction should be recast in accordance with its substance. Thus, internal law principles of the source Contracting State may be applied to identify the beneficial owner of an item of income, and Article 24 then will be applied to the beneficial owner to determine if that person is entitled to the benefits of the Convention with respect to such income.

Paragraph 2

Paragraph 2 has six subparagraphs, each of which describes a category of residents that are entitled to all benefits of the Convention.

It is intended that the provisions of paragraph 2 will be self-executing. Unlike the provisions of paragraph 4, discussed below, claiming benefits under paragraph 2 does not require advance competent authority ruling or approval. The tax authorities may, of course, on review, determine that the taxpayer has improperly interpreted the paragraph and is not entitled to the benefits claimed.

Individuals -- Subparagraph 2(a)

Subparagraph 2(a) provides that individual residents of a Contracting State will be entitled to all treaty benefits. If such an individual receives income as a nominee on behalf of a third country resident, benefits may be denied under the respective articles of the Convention by the requirement that the beneficial owner of the income be a resident of a Contracting State.

Governments -- Subparagraph 2(b)

Subparagraph 2(b) provides that the Contracting States and any political subdivision or local authority or any agency or instrumentality thereof will be entitled to all benefits of the Convention.

Publicly-Traded Corporations -- Subparagraph 2(c)(i)

Subparagraph 2(c) applies to two categories of companies: publicly traded companies and subsidiaries of publicly traded companies. A company resident in a Contracting State is entitled to all the benefits of the Convention under subparagraph 2(c)(i) if the principal class of its shares, and any disproportionate class of shares, is regularly traded on one or more recognized stock exchanges, and the company satisfies at least one of the following additional requirements: the company's principal class of shares is primarily traded on one or more recognized stock exchanges located in the Contracting State of which the company is a resident; or the company's primary place of management and control is in its State of residence.

The term "recognized stock exchange" is defined in subparagraph (a) of paragraph 6. It includes (i) the NASDAQ System and any stock exchange registered with the Securities and Exchange Commission as a national securities exchange for purposes of the Securities Exchange Act of 1934, (ii) the "*Bolsa de Comercio,*" "*Bolsa Electrónica de Chile,*" and "*Bolsa de Corredores,*" and any stock exchange recognized by the "*Superintendencia de Valores y Seguros*" according to Law No. 18.0845, and (iii) any other stock exchanges agreed upon by the competent authorities of the Contracting States.

If a company has only one class of shares, it is only necessary to consider whether the shares of that class meet the relevant trading requirements. If the company has more than one class of shares, it is necessary as an initial matter to determine which class or classes constitute the "principal class of shares." The term "principal class of shares" is defined in subparagraph 6(b) to mean the ordinary or common shares of the company representing the majority of the aggregate voting power and value of the company. If the company does not have a class of ordinary or common shares representing the majority of the aggregate voting power and value of the company, then the "principal class of shares" is that class or any combination of classes of shares that represents, in the aggregate, a majority of the voting power and value of the company. Although in a particular case involving a company with several classes of shares it is conceivable that more than one group of classes could be identified that account for more than 50 percent of the shares, it is only necessary for one such group to satisfy the requirements of this subparagraph in order for the company to be entitled to benefits. Benefits would not be denied to the company even if a second, non-qualifying, group of shares with more than half of the company's voting power and value could be identified.

A company whose principal class of shares is regularly traded on a recognized stock exchange will nevertheless not qualify for benefits under subparagraph 2(c)(i) if it has a disproportionate class of shares that is not regularly traded on a recognized stock exchange. The term "disproportionate class of shares" is defined in subparagraph 7(c). A company has a disproportionate class of shares if it has outstanding a class of shares which is subject to terms or other arrangements that entitle the holder to a larger portion of the company's income, profit, or gain in the other Contracting State than that to which the holder would be entitled in the absence of such terms or arrangements. Thus, for example, a company resident in Chile meets the test of subparagraph 6(c) if it has outstanding a class of "tracking stock" that pays dividends based upon a formula that approximates the company's return on its assets employed in the United States.

The following example illustrates this result.

Example. CCo is a corporation resident in Chile. CCo has two classes of shares: Common and Preferred. The Common shares are listed and regularly traded on the *Bolsa de Comercio*, a recognized Chilean stock exchange. The Preferred shares have no voting rights and are entitled to receive dividends equal in amount to interest payments that CCo receives from unrelated borrowers in the United States. The Preferred shares are owned entirely by a single investor that is a resident of a country with which the United States does not have a tax treaty. The Common shares account for more than 50 percent of the value of CCo and for 100 percent of the voting power. Because the owner of the Preferred shares is entitled to receive payments corresponding to the U.S. source interest income earned by CCo, the Preferred shares are a disproportionate class of shares. Because the Preferred shares are not regularly traded on a recognized stock exchange, CCo will not qualify for benefits under subparagraph 2(c)(i).

The term "regularly traded" is not defined in the Convention. In accordance with paragraph 2 of Article 3 (General Definitions), this term will be defined by reference to the domestic tax laws of the State from which treaty benefits are sought. In the case of the United States, this term is understood to have the meaning it has under Treas. Reg. § 1.884-5(d)(4)(i)(B), relating to the branch tax provisions of the Code. Under these regulations, a class of shares is considered to be "regularly traded" if two requirements are met: trades in the class of shares are made in more than *de minimis* quantities on at least 60 days during the taxable year; and the aggregate number of shares in the class traded during the year is at least 10 percent of the average number of shares outstanding during the year. Treas. Reg. § 1.884-5(d)(4)(i)(A), (ii) and (iii) will not be taken into account for purposes of defining the term "regularly traded" under the Convention.

The regular trading requirement can be met by trading on any recognized exchange or exchanges located in either State. Trading on one or more recognized stock exchanges may be aggregated for purposes of this requirement. Thus, a U.S. company could satisfy the regularly traded requirement through trading, in whole or in part, on a recognized stock exchange located in Chile. Authorized but unissued shares are not considered for purposes of this test.

The term "primarily traded" is not defined in the Convention. In accordance with paragraph 2 of Article 3, this term will have the meaning it has under the laws of the State concerning the taxes to which the Convention applies, generally the source State. In the case of the United States, this term is understood to have the meaning it has under Treas. Reg. § 1.884-5(d)(3), relating to the branch tax provisions of the Code. Accordingly, stock of a corporation is "primarily traded" if the number of shares in the company's principal class of shares that are traded during the taxable year on all recognized stock exchanges in the Contracting State of which the company is a resident exceeds the number of shares in the company's principal class of shares that are traded during that year on established securities markets in any other single foreign country.

A company whose principal class of shares is regularly traded on a recognized exchange but cannot meet the primarily traded test may claim treaty benefits if its primary place of management and control is in its country of residence. This test should be distinguished from the "place of effective management" test which is used in the OECD Model and by many other countries to establish residence. In some cases, the place of effective management test has been interpreted to mean the place where the board of directors meets. By contrast, the primary place of management and control test looks to where day-to-day responsibility for the management of the company (and its subsidiaries) is exercised. The company's primary place of management and control will be located in the State in which the company is a resident only if the executive officers and senior management employees exercise day-to-day responsibility for more of the strategic, financial and operational policy decision making for the company (including direct and indirect subsidiaries) in that State than in the other State or any third state, and the staff that support the management in making those decisions are also based in that State. Thus, the test looks to the overall activities of the relevant persons to see where those activities are conducted.

In most cases, it will be a necessary, but not a sufficient, condition that the headquarters of the company (that is, the place at which the Chief Executive Officer and other top executives normally are based) be located in the Contracting State of which the company is a resident.

To apply the test, it will be necessary to determine which persons are to be considered "executive officers and senior management employees." In most cases, it will not be necessary to look beyond the executives who are members of the board of directors (the "inside directors") in the case of a U.S. company. That will not always be the case, however; in fact, the relevant persons may be employees of subsidiaries if those persons make the strategic, financial and operational policy decisions. Moreover, it would be necessary to take into account any special voting arrangements that result in certain board members making certain decisions without the participation of other board members.

Subsidiaries of Publicly-Traded Corporations -- Subparagraph 2(c)(ii)

A company resident in a Contracting State is entitled to all the benefits of the Convention under subparagraph 2(c)(ii) if five or fewer publicly traded companies described in subparagraph 2(c)(i) are the direct or indirect owners of at least 50 percent of the aggregate vote and value of the company's shares (and at least 50 percent of any disproportionate class of shares). If the publicly-traded companies are indirect owners, however, each of the intermediate companies must be a resident of one of the Contracting States.

Thus, for example, a company that is a resident of Chile, all the shares of which are owned by another company that is a resident of Chile, would qualify for benefits under subparagraph 2(c) if the principal class of shares (and any disproportionate classes of shares) of the parent company are regularly and primarily traded on a recognized stock exchange in Chile. However, such a subsidiary would not qualify for benefits under clause (ii) if the publicly traded parent company were a resident of a third state, for example, and not a resident of the United States or Chile. Furthermore, if a parent company in Chile indirectly owned the bottom-tier company through a chain of subsidiaries, each such subsidiary in the chain, as an intermediate owner, must be a resident of the United States or Chile in order for the subsidiary to meet the test in clause (ii).

Headquarters Companies -- Subparagraph 2(d)

Subparagraph 2(d) provides that a resident of one of the Contracting States is entitled to all the benefits of the Convention if that person functions as a recognized headquarters company for a multinational corporate group. The provisions of this paragraph are consistent with the other U.S. tax treaties where this provision has been adopted. For this purpose, the multinational corporate group includes all corporations that the headquarters company supervises and excludes affiliated corporations not supervised by the headquarters company. The headquarters company does not have to own shares in the companies that it supervises. In order to be considered a headquarters company, the person must meet several requirements that are enumerated in subparagraph 2(d). These requirements are discussed below.

Overall Supervision and Administration

Clause (i) of subparagraph 2(d) provides that the person must provide a substantial portion of the overall supervision and administration of the group. This activity may include group financing, but group financing may not be the principal activity of the person functioning as the headquarters company. A person only will be considered to engage in supervision and administration if it engages in a number of the following activities: group financing, pricing, marketing, internal auditing, internal communications, and management. Other activities also could be part of the function of supervision and administration.

In determining whether a "substantial portion" of the overall supervision and administration of the group is provided by the headquarters company, its headquarters-related activities must be substantial in relation to the same activities for the same group performed by other entities. Clause (i) does not require that the group that is supervised include persons in the other State. However, it is anticipated that in most cases the group will include such persons, due to the requirement in subparagraph 2(d)(vii), discussed below, that the income derived in the other Contracting State by the headquarters company be derived in connection with or be incidental to an active trade or business supervised by the headquarters company.

78

Clause (ii) of subparagraph 2(d) is the first of several requirements intended to ensure that the relevant group is truly "multinational." This subparagraph provides that the corporate group supervised by the headquarters company must consist of corporations resident in, and engaged in active trades or businesses in, at least five countries. Furthermore, at least five countries must each contribute substantially to the income generated by the group, as the rule requires that the business activities carried on in each of the five countries (or groupings of countries) generate at least 10 percent of the gross income of the group. For purposes of the 10 percent gross income requirement, the income from multiple countries may be aggregated into non-overlapping groupings, as long as there are at least five individual countries or groupings that each satisfies the 10 percent requirement. If the gross income requirement under this subparagraph is not met for a taxable year, the taxpayer may satisfy this requirement by applying the 10 percent gross income test to the average of the gross incomes for the four years preceding the taxable year.

Example. CHQ is a corporation resident in Chile. CHQ functions as a headquarters company for a group of companies. These companies are resident in the United States, Canada, New Zealand, the United Kingdom, Malaysia, the Philippines, Singapore, and Indonesia. The gross income generated by each of these companies for 2012 and 2013 is as follows:

Country	2012	2013
United States	$40	$45
Canada	$25	$15
New Zealand	$10	$20
United Kingdom	$30	$35
Malaysia	$10	$12
Philippines	$7	$10
Singapore	$10	$8
Indonesia	$5	$10
Total	$137	$155

For 2012, 10 percent of the gross income of this group is equal to $13.70. Only the United States, Canada, and the United Kingdom satisfy this requirement for that year. The other countries may be aggregated to meet this requirement. Because New Zealand and Malaysia have a total gross income of $20, and the Philippines, Singapore, and Indonesia have a total gross income of $22, these two groupings of countries may be treated as the fourth and fifth members of the group for purposes of clause (ii).

In the following year, 10 percent of the gross income is $15.50. Only the United States, New Zealand, and the United Kingdom satisfy this requirement. Because Canada and Malaysia have a total gross income of $27, and the Philippines, Singapore, and Indonesia have a total gross income of $28, these two groupings of countries may be treated as the fourth and fifth members of the group for purposes of clause (ii). The fact that Canada replaced New Zealand in a group is not relevant for this purpose. The composition of the grouping may change from year to year.

Single Country Limitation

Clause (iii) of subparagraph 2(d) provides that the business activities carried on in any one country other than the headquarters company's State of residence must generate less than 50 percent of the gross income of the group. If the gross income requirement under this subparagraph is not met for a taxable year, the taxpayer may satisfy this requirement by applying the 50 percent gross income test to the average of the gross incomes for the four years preceding the taxable year. The following example illustrates the application of this clause.

Example. CHQ is a corporation resident in Chile. CHQ functions as a headquarters company for a group of companies. CHQ derives dividend income from a United States subsidiary in the 2008 taxable year. The state of residence of each of these companies, the situs of their activities and the amounts of gross income attributable to each for the years 2012 through 2016 are set forth below.

Country	Situs	2012	2011	2010	2009	2008
United States	U.S.	$100	$100	$95	$90	$85
Mexico	U.S.	$10	$8	$5	$0	$0
Canada	U.S.	$20	$18	$16	$15	$12
United Kingdom	U.K	$30	$32	$30	$28	$27
New Zealand	N.Z.	$35	$42	$38	$36	$35
Japan	Japan	$35	$32	$30	$30	$28
Singapore	Singapore	$30	$25	$24	$22	$20
Total		$260	$257	$238	$221	$207

Because the United States' total gross income of $130 in 2012 is not less than 50 percent of the gross income of the group, clause (iii) is not satisfied with respect to dividends derived in 2012. However, the United States' average gross income for the preceding four years may be used in lieu of the preceding year's average. The United States' average gross income for the years 2008-11 is $111.00 ($444/4). The group's total average gross income for these years is $230.75 ($923/4). Because $111 represents 48.1 percent of the group's average gross income for the years 2008 through 2011, the requirement under clause (iii) is satisfied.

Other State Gross Income Limitation

Clause (iv) of subparagraph 2(d) provides that no more than 25 percent of the headquarters company's gross income may be derived from the other Contracting State. Thus, if the headquarters company's gross income for the taxable year is $200, no more than $50 of this amount may be derived from the other Contracting State. If the gross income requirement under this subparagraph is not met for a taxable year, the taxpayer may satisfy this requirement by applying the 25 percent gross income test to the average of the gross incomes for the four years preceding the taxable year.

Independent Discretionary Authority

Clause (v) of subparagraph 2(d) requires that the headquarters company have and exercise independent discretionary authority to carry out the functions referred to in clause (i). Thus, if the headquarters company was nominally responsible for group financing, pricing, marketing and other management functions, but merely implemented instructions received from another entity, the headquarters company would not be considered to have and exercise independent discretionary authority with respect to these functions. This determination is made individually for each function. For instance, a headquarters company could be nominally responsible for group financing, pricing, marketing and internal auditing functions, but another entity could be actually directing the headquarters company as to the group financing function. In such a case, the headquarters company would not be deemed to have independent discretionary authority for group financing, but it might have such authority for the other functions. Functions for which the headquarters company does not have and exercise independent discretionary authority are considered to be conducted by an entity other than the headquarters company for purposes of clause (i).

Income Taxation Rules

Clause (vi) of subparagraph 2(d) requires that the headquarters company be subject to the generally applicable income taxation rules in its country of residence. This reference should be understood to mean that the company must be subject to the income taxation rules to which a company engaged in the active conduct of a trade or business would be subject. Thus, if one of the Contracting States has or introduces special taxation legislation that imposes a lower rate of income tax on headquarters companies than is imposed on companies engaged in the active conduct of a trade or business, or provides for an artificially low taxable base for such companies, a headquarters company subject to these rules is not entitled to the benefits of the Convention under subparagraph 2(d).

In Connection With or Incidental to Trade or Business

Clause (vii) of subparagraph 2(d) requires that the income derived in the other Contracting State be derived in connection with or be incidental to the active business activities referred to in clause (ii). This determination is made under the principles set forth in paragraph 3. For instance, assume that a Chilean company satisfies the other requirements in subparagraph 2(d) and acts as a headquarters company for a group that includes a U.S. corporation. If the group is engaged in the design and manufacture of computer software, but the U.S. corporation is also engaged in the design and manufacture of photocopying machines, the income that the Chilean company derives from the United States would have to be derived in connection with or be incidental to the income generated by the computer business in order to be entitled to the benefits of the Convention under subparagraph 2(d). Interest income received from the U.S. corporation also would be entitled to the benefits of the Convention under this subparagraph as long as the interest was attributable to the computer business supervised by the headquarters company. Interest income derived from an unrelated party would normally not, however, satisfy the requirements of this clause.

Tax Exempt Organizations – Subparagraph 2(e)

Subparagraph 2(e) provides rules by which tax exempt organizations will be entitled to all the benefits of the Convention. Entities qualifying under this rule are those that are generally exempt from tax in their State of residence and that are organized and operated exclusively to fulfill religious, charitable, scientific, artistic, cultural, or educational purposes.

Pension Funds – Subparagraph 2(f)

A pension fund will qualify for benefits under subparagraph 2(f), if in the case of a person described in subclause (A) of clause (ii) of subparagraph (j) of paragraph 1 of Article 3 (General Definitions), more than 50 percent of the beneficiaries, members or participants of the pension fund are individuals resident in either Contracting State. For purposes of this provision, the term "beneficiaries" should be understood to refer to the persons receiving benefits from the organization.

Ownership/Base Erosion -- Subparagraph 2(g)

Subparagraph 2(g) provides an additional method to qualify for treaty benefits that applies to any form of legal entity that is a resident of a Contracting State. The test provided in this subparagraph, the so-called ownership and base erosion test, is a two-part test. Both prongs of the test must be satisfied for the resident to be entitled to treaty benefits under subparagraph 2(g).

The ownership prong of the test, under clause (i), requires that shares or other beneficial interests representing at least 50 percent of the aggregate voting power and value (and at least 50 percent of any disproportionate class of shares) of the person be owned, directly or indirectly, on at least half the days of the person's taxable year by persons who are residents of the Contracting State of which that person is a resident and that are themselves entitled to treaty benefits under subparagraph 2(a), 2(b), 2(c)(i), 2(e) or 2(f). In the case of indirect owners, each of the intermediate owners must be a resident of that Contracting State.

Trusts may be entitled to benefits under this provision if they are treated as residents under Article 4 (Residence) and they otherwise satisfy the requirements of this subparagraph. For purposes of this subparagraph, the beneficial interests in a trust will be considered to be owned by its beneficiaries in proportion to each beneficiary's actuarial interest in the trust. The interest of a remainder beneficiary will be equal to 100 percent less the aggregate percentages held by income beneficiaries. A beneficiary's interest in a trust will not be considered to be owned by a person entitled to benefits under the other provisions of paragraph 2 if it is not possible to determine the beneficiary's actuarial interest. Consequently, if it is not possible to determine the actuarial interest of the beneficiaries in a trust, the ownership test under clause (i)

82

cannot be satisfied, unless all possible beneficiaries are persons entitled to benefits under subparagraph 2(a), 2(b), 2(c)(i), 2(e) or 2(f).

The base erosion prong of clause (ii) of subparagraph 2(g) is satisfied with respect to a person if less than 50 percent of the person's gross income for the taxable year, as determined under the tax law in the person's State of residence, is paid or accrued, directly or indirectly, to persons who are not residents of either Contracting State entitled to benefits under subparagraph 2(a), 2(b), 2(c)(i), 2(e) or 2(f), in the form of payments deductible for tax purposes in the payor's State of residence. These amounts do not include arm's-length payments in the ordinary course of business for services or tangible property. To the extent they are deductible from the taxable base, trust distributions are deductible payments. However, depreciation and amortization deductions, which do not represent payments or accruals to other persons, are disregarded for this purpose.

Paragraph 3

Paragraph 3 sets forth an alternative test under which a resident of a Contracting State may receive treaty benefits with respect to certain items of income that are connected to an active trade or business conducted in its State of residence. A resident of a Contracting State may qualify for benefits under paragraph 3 even though it does not qualify under paragraph 2.

Subparagraph 3(a) sets forth the general rule that a resident of a Contracting State engaged in the active conduct of a trade or business in that State may obtain the benefits of the Convention with respect to an item of income derived in the other Contracting State. The item of income, however, must be derived in connection with or incidental to that trade or business.

The term "trade or business" is not defined in the Convention. Pursuant to paragraph 2 of Article 3 (General Definitions), when determining whether a resident of Chile is entitled to the benefits of the Convention under paragraph 3 of this Article with respect to an item of income derived from sources within the United States, the United States will ascribe to this term the meaning that it has under the law of the United States. Accordingly, the U.S. competent authority will refer to the regulations issued under section 367(a) for the definition of the term "trade or business." In general, therefore, a trade or business will be considered to be a specific unified group of activities that constitutes or could constitute an independent economic enterprise carried on for profit. Furthermore, a corporation generally will be considered to carry on a trade or business only if the officers and employees of the corporation conduct substantial managerial and operational activities.

The business of making or managing investments for the resident's own account will be considered to be a trade or business only when part of banking, insurance or securities activities conducted by a bank, insurance company or registered securities dealer. Such activities conducted by a person other than a bank, insurance company, or registered securities dealer will not be considered to be the conduct of an active trade or business, nor would they be considered to be the conduct of an active trade or business if conducted by a bank, insurance company or registered securities dealer but not as part of the company's banking, insurance, or dealer business. Because a headquarters operation is in the business of managing investments, a company that functions solely as a headquarters company will not be considered to be engaged in an active trade or business for purposes of paragraph 3.

An item of income is derived in connection with a trade or business if the income-producing activity in the State of source is a line of business that "forms a part of" or is "complementary" to the trade or business conducted in the State of residence by the income recipient.

A business activity generally will be considered to form part of a business activity conducted in the State of source if the two activities involve the design, manufacture or sale of the same products or type of products, or the provision of similar services. The line of business in the State of residence may be upstream, downstream, or parallel to the activity conducted in the State of source. Thus, the line of business may provide inputs for a manufacturing process that occurs in the State of source, may sell the output of that manufacturing process, or simply may sell the same sorts of products that are being sold by the trade or business carried on in the State of source.

Example 1. USCo is a corporation resident in the United States. USCo is engaged in an active manufacturing business in the United States. USCo owns 100 percent of the shares of CCo, a corporation resident in Chile. CCo distributes USCo products in Chile. Since the business activities conducted by the two corporations involve the same products, CCo's distribution business is considered to form a part of USCo's manufacturing business.

Example 2. The facts are the same as in Example 1, except that USCo does not manufacture. Rather, USCo operates a large research and development facility in the United States that licenses intellectual property to affiliates worldwide, including CCo. CCo and other USCo affiliates then manufacture and market the USCo-designed products in their respective markets. Since the activities conducted by CCo and USCo involve the same product lines, these activities are considered to form a part of the same trade or business.

For two activities to be considered to be "complementary," the activities need not relate to the same types of products or services, but they should be part of the same overall industry and be related in the sense that the success or failure of one activity will tend to result in success or failure for the other. Where more than one trade or business is conducted in the State of source and only one of the trades or businesses forms a part of or is complementary to a trade or business conducted in the State of residence, it is necessary to identify the trade or business to which an item of income is attributable. Royalties generally will be considered to be derived in connection with the trade or business to which the underlying intangible property is attributable. Dividends will be deemed to be derived first out of earnings and profits of the treaty-benefited trade or business, and then out of other earnings and profits. Interest income may be allocated under any reasonable method consistently applied. A method that conforms to U.S. principles for expense allocation will be considered a reasonable method.

Example 3. Americair is a corporation resident in the United States that operates an international airline. CSub is a wholly-owned subsidiary of Americair resident in Chile. CSub operates a chain of hotels in Chile that are located near airports served by Americair flights. Americair frequently sells tour packages that include air travel to Chile and lodging at CSub hotels. Although both companies are engaged in the active conduct of a trade or business, the businesses of operating a chain of hotels and operating an airline are distinct trades or businesses. Therefore CSub's business does not form a part of Americair's business. However, CSub's business is considered to be complementary to Americair's business because they are part of the same overall industry (travel) and the links between their operations tend to make them interdependent.

Example 4. The facts are the same as in Example 3, except that CSub owns an office building in Chile instead of a hotel chain. No part of Americair's business is conducted through the office building. CSub's business is not considered to form a part of or to be complementary to Americair's business. They are engaged in distinct trades or businesses in separate industries, and there is no economic dependence between the two operations.

Example 5. USFlower is a corporation resident in the United States. USFlower produces and sells flowers in the United States and other countries. USFlower owns all the shares of CHolding, a corporation resident in Chile. CHolding is a holding company that is not engaged in a trade or business. CHolding owns all the shares of three corporations that are resident in Chile: CFlower, CLawn, and CFish. CFlower distributes USFlower flowers under the USFlower trademark in Chile. CLawn markets a line of lawn care products in Chile under the USFlower trademark. In addition to being sold under the same trademark, CLawn and CFlower products are sold in the same stores and sales of each company's products tend to generate increased sales of the other's products. CFish imports fish from the United States and distributes it to fish wholesalers in Chile. For purposes of paragraph 3, the business of CFlower forms a part of the business of USFlower, the business of CLawn is complementary to the business of USFlower, and the business of CFish is neither part of nor complementary to that of USFlower.

An item of income derived from the State of source is "incidental to" the trade or business carried on in the State of residence if production of the item facilitates the conduct of the trade or business in the State of residence. An example of incidental income is the temporary investment of working capital of a person in the State of residence in securities issued by persons in the State of source.

Subparagraph 3(b) states a further condition to the general rule in subparagraph 3(a) in cases where the trade or business generating the item of income in question is carried on either by the person deriving the income or by any associated enterprises. Subparagraph 3(b) states that the trade or business carried on in the State of residence, under these circumstances, must be substantial in relation to the activity in the State of source. The substantiality requirement is intended to prevent a narrow case of treaty-shopping abuses in which a company attempts to qualify for benefits by engaging in de minimis connected business activities in the treaty country in which it is resident (i.e., activities that have little economic cost or effect with respect to the company business as a whole).

The determination of substantiality is made based upon all the facts and circumstances and takes into account the comparative sizes of the trades or businesses in each Contracting State, the nature of the activities performed in each Contracting State, and the relative contributions made to that trade or business in each Contracting State.

The determination in subparagraph 3(b) is also made separately for each item of income derived from the State of source. It therefore is possible that a person would be entitled to the benefits of the Convention with respect to one item of income but not with respect to another. If a resident of a Contracting State is entitled to treaty benefits with respect to a particular item of income under paragraph 3, the resident is entitled to all benefits of the Convention insofar as they affect the taxation of that item of income in the State of source.

The application of the substantiality requirement only to income from related parties focuses only on potential abuse cases, and does not hamper certain other kinds of non-abusive activities, even though the income recipient resident in a Contracting State may be very small in relation to the entity generating income in the other Contracting State. For example, if a small U.S. research firm develops a process that it licenses to a very large, unrelated, pharmaceutical manufacturer in Chile, the size of the U.S. research firm would not have to be tested against the size of the manufacturer. Similarly, a small U.S. bank that makes a loan to a very large unrelated company operating a business in Chile would not have to pass a substantiality test to receive treaty benefits under paragraph 3.

Subparagraph 3(c) provides special attribution rules for purposes of applying the substantive rules of subparagraphs 3(a) and 3(b). Thus, these rules apply for purposes of determining whether a person meets the requirement in subparagraph 3(a) that it be engaged in the active conduct of a trade or business and that the item of income is derived in connection with that active trade or business, and for making the comparison required by the "substantiality" requirement in subparagraph 3(b). Subparagraph (c) attributes to a person activities conducted by persons "connected" to such person. A person ("X") is connected to another person ("Y") if X possesses 50 percent or more of the beneficial interest in Y (or if Y possesses 50 percent or more of the beneficial interest in X). For this purpose, X is connected to a company if X owns shares representing 50 percent or more of the aggregate voting power and value of the company or 50 percent or more of the beneficial equity interest in the company. X also is connected to Y if a third person possesses 50 percent or more of the beneficial interest in both X and Y. For this purpose, if X or Y is a company, the threshold relationship with respect to such company or companies is 50 percent or more of the aggregate voting power and value or 50 percent or more of the beneficial equity interest. Finally, X is connected to Y if, based upon all the facts and circumstances, X controls Y, Y controls X, or X and Y are controlled by the same person or persons.

Paragraph 4

Paragraph 4 provides that a resident of one of the States that is not entitled to the benefits of the Convention as a result of paragraph 2 or 3 still may be granted benefits under the Convention at the discretion of the competent authority of the State from which benefits are claimed. Under paragraph 4, that competent authority will determine whether the establishment, acquisition or maintenance of the person seeking benefits under the Convention, or the conduct of such person's operations, has or had as one of its principal purposes the obtaining of benefits under the Convention. Benefits will not be granted, however, solely because a company was established prior to the effective date of a treaty or protocol. In that case a company would still be required to establish to the satisfaction of the competent authority clear non-tax business reasons for its formation in a Contracting State, or that the allowance of benefits would not otherwise be contrary to the purposes of the treaty. Thus, persons that establish operations in one of the States with a principal purpose of obtaining the benefits of the Convention ordinarily will not be granted relief under paragraph 4.

The competent authority's discretion is quite broad. It may grant all of the benefits of the Convention to the taxpayer making the request, or it may grant only certain benefits. For instance, it may grant benefits only with respect to a particular item of income in a manner similar to paragraph 4. Further, the competent authority may establish conditions, such as setting time limits on the duration of any relief granted.

For purposes of implementing paragraph 4, a taxpayer will be permitted to present his case to the relevant competent authority for an advance determination based on the facts. In these circumstances, it is also expected that, if the competent authority determines that benefits are to be allowed, they will be allowed retroactively to the time of entry into force of the relevant treaty provision or the establishment of the structure in question, whichever is later.

Finally, there may be cases in which a resident of a Contracting State may apply for discretionary relief to the competent authority of his State of residence. This would arise, for example, if the benefit the resident is claiming is provided by the residence State, and not by the source State. So, for example, if a company that is a resident of the United States would like to claim the benefit of the re-sourcing rule of paragraph 3 of Article 23, but it does not meet any of the objective tests of this Article, it may apply to the U.S. competent authority for discretionary relief.

Paragraph 5

Paragraph 5 deals with the treatment of income in the context of a so-called "triangular case." An example of a triangular case would be a structure under which a resident of Chile earns interest income from the United States. The resident of Chile, who is assumed to qualify for benefits under one or more of the provisions of this Article, sets up a permanent establishment in a third jurisdiction that imposes only a low rate of tax on the income of the permanent establishment. The Chilean resident lends funds into the United States through the permanent establishment. The permanent establishment, despite its third-jurisdiction location, is an integral part of a Chilean resident. Therefore, the income that it earns on those loans, absent the provisions of paragraph 5, is entitled to a reduced rate of withholding tax under the Convention. Under a current Chilean income tax treaty with the host jurisdiction of the permanent establishment, the income of the permanent establishment is exempt from Chilean tax (alternatively, Chile may choose to exempt the income of the permanent establishment from

Chilean income tax by statute). In addition, the third jurisdiction may exempt the income of the permanent establishment, for example by statute or ruling. Thus, the interest income is exempt from U.S. tax, is subject to little tax in the host jurisdiction of the permanent establishment, and is exempt from Chilean tax.

Paragraph 5 applies reciprocally. However, the United States does not exempt the profits of a third-jurisdiction permanent establishment of a U.S. resident from U.S. tax, either by statute or by treaty.

Paragraph 5 provides that the tax benefits that would otherwise apply under the Convention will not apply to any item of income if the combined tax actually paid in the residence State and the third state is less than 60 percent of the tax that would have been payable in the residence State if the income were earned in that State by the enterprise and were not attributable to the permanent establishment in the third state. In the case of dividends, interest and royalties to which this paragraph applies, the withholding tax rates under the Convention are replaced with a 15 percent withholding tax. Any other income to which the provisions of paragraph 5 apply is subject to tax under the domestic law of the source State, notwithstanding any other provisions of the Convention.

In general, the principles employed under Code section 954(b)(4) will be employed to determine whether the profits are subject to an effective rate of taxation that is above the specified threshold.

Notwithstanding the level of tax on interest and royalty income of the permanent establishment, paragraph 5 will not apply under certain circumstances. In the case of royalties, paragraph 5 will not apply if the royalties are received as compensation for the use of, or the right to use, intangible property produced or developed by the permanent establishment itself. In the case of any other income, paragraph 5 will not apply if that income is derived in connection with, or is incidental to, the active conduct of a trade or business carried on by the permanent establishment in the third state. The business of making, managing or simply holding investments for the enterprise's own account is not considered to be an active trade or business, unless these are banking or securities activities carried on by a bank or registered securities dealer.

Paragraph 6

Paragraph 6 defines several key terms for purposes of Article 24. Each of the defined terms is discussed above in the context in which it is used.

ARTICLE 25 (NON-DISCRIMINATION)

This Article ensures that nationals of a Contracting State, in the case of paragraph 1, and residents of a Contracting State, in the case of paragraphs 2 through 4, will not be subject, directly or indirectly, to discriminatory taxation in the other Contracting State. Not all differences in tax treatment, either as between nationals of the two States, or between residents of the two States, are violations of the prohibition against discrimination. Rather, the non-discrimination obligations of this Article apply only if the nationals or residents of the two States are comparably situated.

Each of the relevant paragraphs of the Article provides that two persons that are comparably situated must be treated similarly. Although the actual words differ from paragraph to paragraph (*e.g.*, paragraph 1 refers to two nationals "in the same circumstances," paragraph 2 refers to two enterprises "carrying on the same activities" and paragraph 4 refers to two companies that are "similar"), the common underlying premise is that if the difference in treatment is directly related to a tax-relevant difference in the situations of the domestic and foreign persons being compared, that difference is not to be treated as discriminatory (*i.e.*, if one person is taxable in a Contracting State on worldwide income and the other is not, or tax may be collectible from one person at a later stage, but not from the other, distinctions in treatment would be justified under paragraph 1). Other examples of such factors that can lead to non-discriminatory differences in treatment are noted in the discussions of each paragraph.

The operative paragraphs of the Article also use different language to identify the kinds of differences in taxation treatment that will be considered discriminatory. For example, paragraphs 1 and 4 refer to any taxation that is more burdensome, while paragraph 2 specifies that a tax "shall not be less favorably levied." Regardless of these differences in language, only differences in tax treatment that materially disadvantage the foreign person relative to the domestic person are properly the subject of the Article.

Paragraph 1

Paragraph 1 provides that a national of one Contracting State may not be subject to taxation or connected requirements in the other Contracting State that are other or more burdensome than the taxes and connected requirements imposed upon a national of that other State in the same circumstances.

The term "national" in relation to a Contracting State is defined in subparagraph 1(i) of Article 3 (General Definitions). The term includes both individuals and juridical persons. A national of a Contracting State is afforded protection under this paragraph even if the national is not a resident of either Contracting State. Thus, a U.S. citizen who is resident in a third country is entitled under this paragraph to the same treatment in Chile as a national of Chile who is in similar circumstances (*i.e.*, presumably one who is resident in a third State).

Paragraph 1 specifically states that a citizen or national of a Contracting State who is not a resident of that Contracting State and a citizen or national of the other Contracting State who is not a resident of the first-mentioned State are not in the same circumstances with respect to the tax of that first-mentioned State. Thus, for example, the United States is not obligated to apply the same taxing regime to a national of Chile who is not resident in the United States as it applies to a U.S. national who is not resident in the United States. U.S. citizens who are not residents of the United States but who are nevertheless subject to United States tax on their worldwide income are not in the same circumstances with respect to United States taxation as citizens of

Chile who are not United States residents. Accordingly, Article 25 would not entitle a national of Chile resident in a third country to taxation at graduated rates on U.S. source dividends or other investment income that applies to a U.S. citizen resident in the same third country.

Paragraph 2

Paragraph 2 of the Article provides that a Contracting State may not tax a permanent establishment of an enterprise of the other Contracting State less favorably than an enterprise of that first-mentioned State that is carrying on the same activities.

The fact that a U.S. permanent establishment of an enterprise of Chile is subject to U.S. tax only on income that is attributable to the permanent establishment, while a U.S. corporation engaged in the same activities is taxable on its worldwide income is not, in itself, a sufficient difference to provide different treatment for the permanent establishment. There are cases, however, where the two enterprises would not be similarly situated and differences in treatment may be warranted. For instance, it would not be a violation of the non-discrimination protection of paragraph 2 to require the foreign enterprise to provide information in a reasonable manner that may be different from the information requirements imposed on a resident enterprise, because information may not be as readily available to the Internal Revenue Service from a foreign as from a domestic enterprise. Similarly, it would not be a violation of paragraph 2 to impose penalties on persons who fail to comply with such a requirement (*see, e.g.*, sections 874(a) and 882(c)(2)). Further, a determination that income and expenses have been attributed or allocated to a permanent establishment in conformity with the principles of Article 7 (Business Profits) implies that the attribution or allocation was not discriminatory.

Code section 1446 imposes on any partnership with income that is effectively connected with a U.S. trade or business the obligation to withhold tax on amounts allocable to a foreign partner. In the context of the Convention, this obligation applies with respect to a share of the partnership income of a partner resident in Chile, and attributable to a U.S. permanent establishment. There is no similar obligation with respect to the distributive shares of U.S. resident partners. It is understood, however, that this distinction is not a form of discrimination within the meaning of paragraph 2 of the Article. No distinction is made between U.S. and non-U.S. partnerships, since the law requires that partnerships of both U.S. and non-U.S. domicile withhold tax in respect of the partnership shares of non-U.S. partners. Furthermore, in distinguishing between U.S. and non-U.S. partners, the requirement to withhold on the non-U.S. but not the U.S. partner's share is not discriminatory taxation, but, like other withholding on nonresident aliens, is merely a reasonable method for the collection of tax from persons who are not continually present in the United States, and as to whom it otherwise may be difficult for the United States to enforce its tax jurisdiction. If tax has been over-withheld, the partner can, as in other cases of over-withholding, file for a refund.

Paragraph 2 also makes clear that the provisions of paragraphs 1 and 2 do not obligate a Contracting State to grant to a resident of the other Contracting State any tax allowances, reliefs, etc., that it grants to its own residents on account of their civil status or family responsibilities. Thus, if a sole proprietor who is a resident of Chile has a permanent establishment in the United

States, in assessing income tax on the profits attributable to the permanent establishment, the United States is not obligated to allow to the resident of Chile the personal allowances for himself and his family that he would be permitted to take if the permanent establishment were a sole proprietorship owned and operated by a U.S. resident, despite the fact that the individual income tax rates would apply.

Paragraph 3

Paragraph 3 prohibits discrimination in the allowance of deductions. When a resident or an enterprise of a Contracting State pays interest, royalties or other disbursements to a resident of the other Contracting State, the first-mentioned Contracting State must allow a deduction for those payments in computing the taxable profits of the resident or enterprise as if the payment had been made under the same conditions to a resident of the first-mentioned Contracting State. Paragraph 3, however, does not require a Contracting State to give nonresidents more favorable treatment than it gives to its own residents. Consequently, a Contracting State does not have to allow nonresidents a deduction for items that are not deductible under its domestic law (for example, expenses of a capital nature).

The term "other disbursements" is understood to include a reasonable allocation of executive and general administrative expenses, research and development expenses, and other expenses incurred for the benefit of a group of related persons that includes the person incurring the expense.

An exception to the rule of paragraph 3 is provided for cases where the provisions of paragraph 1 of Article 9 (Associated Enterprises), paragraph 8 of Article 11 (Interest) or paragraph 6 of Article 12 (Royalties) apply. All of these provisions permit the denial of deductions in certain circumstances in respect of transactions between related persons. Neither State is forced to apply the non-discrimination principle in such cases. The exception with respect to paragraph 8 of Article 11 would include the denial or deferral of certain interest deductions under Code section 163(j).

Paragraph 3 also provides that any debts of an enterprise of a Contracting State to a resident of the other Contracting State are deductible in the first-mentioned Contracting State for purposes of computing the capital tax of the enterprise under the same conditions as if the debt had been contracted to a resident of the first-mentioned Contracting State. This provision is relevant for both States as the Convention covers taxes on income and capital, and under paragraph 6 of this Article, the nondiscrimination provisions apply to all taxes levied in both Contracting States at all levels of government. In the United States such taxes frequently are imposed by local governments and the same may be true in the case of Chile.

Paragraph 4

Paragraph 4 requires that a Contracting State not impose more burdensome taxation on a company that is a resident of that State the capital of which is wholly or partly owned or controlled, directly or indirectly, by one or more residents of the other Contracting State than the taxation that it imposes or may impose on other similar companies of that first-mentioned Contracting State. For this purpose it is understood that "similar" refers to similar activities or ownership of the company.

This rule, like all non-discrimination provisions, does not prohibit differing treatment of entities that are in differing circumstances. Rather, a protected enterprise is only required to be treated in the same manner as other enterprises that, from the point of view of the application of the tax law, are in substantially similar circumstances both in law and in fact. The taxation of a distributing corporation under section 367(e) on an applicable distribution to foreign shareholders does not violate paragraph 4 of the Article because a foreign-owned corporation is not similar to a domestically-owned corporation that is accorded non-recognition treatment under sections 337 and 355.

For the reasons given above in connection with the discussion of paragraph 2 of the Article, it is also understood that the provision in Code section 1446 for withholding of tax on non-U.S. partners does not violate paragraph 4 of the Article.

It is further understood that the ineligibility of a U.S. corporation with nonresident alien shareholders to make an election to be an "S" corporation does not violate paragraph 4 of the Article. If a corporation elects to be an S corporation, it is generally not subject to income tax and the shareholders take into account their pro rata shares of the corporation's items of income, loss, deduction or credit. A nonresident alien does not pay U.S. tax on a net basis, and, thus, does not generally take into account items of loss, deduction or credit. Thus, the S corporation provisions do not exclude corporations with nonresident alien shareholders because such shareholders are foreign, but only because they are not net-basis taxpayers. Similarly, the provisions exclude corporations with other types of shareholders where the purpose of the provisions cannot be fulfilled or their mechanics implemented. For example, corporations with corporate shareholders are excluded because the purpose of the provision to permit individuals to conduct a business in corporate form at individual tax rates would not be furthered by their inclusion.

Finally, it is understood that paragraph 4 does not require a Contracting State to allow foreign corporations to join in filing a consolidated return with a domestic corporation or to allow similar benefits between domestic and foreign enterprises.

Paragraph 5

Paragraph 5 of the Article confirms that no provision of the Article will prevent either Contracting State from imposing the branch profits tax described in paragraph 7 of Article 10 (Dividends) or the branch level interest tax described in paragraph 10 of Article 11 (Interest).

Paragraph 6

As noted above, notwithstanding the specification of taxes covered by the Convention in Article 2 (Taxes Covered) for general purposes, for purposes of providing nondiscrimination protection this Article applies to taxes of every kind and description imposed by a Contracting State or a political subdivision or local authority thereof. However, in the case of taxes not covered by the Convention, the provisions of this Article shall not apply to any taxation laws of a Contracting State that were in force on February 4, 2010, the date of signature of the Convention. Customs duties are not considered to be taxes for purposes of this Article.

Relationship to Other Articles

The saving clause of paragraph 4 of the Protocol does not apply to this Article by virtue of the exception for Article 25 in that paragraph. Thus, for example, a U.S. citizen who is a resident of Chile may claim benefits in the United States under this Article.

Nationals of a Contracting State may claim the benefits of paragraph 1 regardless of whether they are entitled to benefits under Article 24 (Limitation on Benefits), because that paragraph applies to nationals and not residents. They may not claim the benefits of the other paragraphs of this Article with respect to an item of income unless they are generally entitled to treaty benefits with respect to that income under a provision of Article 24.

ARTICLE 26 (MUTUAL AGREEMENT PROCEDURE)

This Article provides the mechanism for taxpayers to bring to the attention of competent authorities issues and problems that may arise under the Convention. It also provides the authority for cooperation between the competent authorities of the Contracting States to resolve disputes and clarify issues that may arise under the Convention and to resolve cases of double taxation not provided for in the Convention. The competent authorities of the two Contracting States are identified in subparagraph 1(h) of Article 3 (General Definitions).

Paragraph 1

This paragraph provides that, where a resident of a Contracting State considers that the actions of one or both Contracting States will result in taxation that is not in accordance with the Convention, he may present his case to the competent authority of the Contracting State of which he is resident, or, if his case comes under paragraph 1 of Article 25 (Non-Discrimination), to the competent authority of the State of which he is a national.

Although the most common cases brought under this paragraph will involve economic double taxation arising from transfer pricing adjustments, the scope of this paragraph is not limited to such cases. For example, a taxpayer could request assistance from the competent authority if one Contracting State determines that the taxpayer has received deferred compensation taxable at source under Article 15 (Dependent Personal Services), while the taxpayer believes that such income should be treated as a pension that is taxable only in his country of residence pursuant to Article 18 (Pensions, Social Security, Alimony and Child Support).

It is not necessary for a person requesting assistance first to have exhausted the remedies provided under the national laws of the Contracting States before presenting a case to the competent authorities, nor does the fact that the statute of limitations may have passed for seeking a refund preclude bringing a case to the competent authority. The case must be presented within three years from the first notification of the action resulting in taxation not in accordance with the provisions of the Convention.

Paragraph 2

Paragraph 2 sets out the framework within which the competent authorities will deal with cases brought by taxpayers under paragraph 1. It provides that, if the competent authority of the Contracting State to which the case is presented judges the case to have merit and cannot reach a unilateral solution, it shall seek an agreement with the competent authority of the other Contracting State pursuant to which taxation not in accordance with the Convention will be avoided.

Any agreement is to be implemented even if such implementation otherwise would be barred by the statute of limitations or by some other procedural limitation, such as a closing agreement. Paragraph 2, however, does not prevent the application of domestic-law procedural limitations that give effect to the agreement (*e.g.*, a domestic-law requirement that the taxpayer file a return reflecting the agreement within one year of the date of the agreement).

Where the taxpayer has entered a closing agreement (or other written settlement) with the United States before bringing a case to the competent authorities, the U.S. competent authority will endeavor only to obtain a correlative adjustment from Chile. *See* Rev. Proc. 2006-54, 2006-49 I.R.B. 1035, § 7.05. Because, as specified in paragraph 2 of the Protocol, the Convention cannot operate to increase a taxpayer's liability, temporal or other procedural limitations can be overridden only for the purpose of making refunds and not to impose additional tax.

Paragraph 3

Paragraph 3 authorizes the competent authorities to resolve by mutual agreement any difficulties or doubts that may arise as to the application or interpretation of the Convention.

The competent authorities may, for example, agree to the same allocation of income, deductions, credits or allowances between an enterprise in one Contracting State and its permanent establishment in the other or between related persons. These allocations are to be made in accordance with the arm's length principle underlying Article 7 (Business Profits) and Article 9 (Associated Enterprises). Agreements reached under Article 26 may include agreement on a methodology for determining an appropriate transfer price, on an acceptable range of results under that methodology, or on a common treatment of a taxpayer's cost sharing arrangement.

The competent authorities also may agree to settle a variety of conflicting applications of the Convention. They may agree to settle conflicts regarding the characterization of particular items of income, the characterization of persons, the application of source rules to particular items of income, the meaning of a term, or the timing of an item of income.

The competent authorities also may agree as to advance pricing arrangements. They also may agree as to the application of the provisions of domestic law regarding penalties, fines, and interest in a manner consistent with the purposes of the Convention.

The competent authorities may also, for example, seek agreement on a uniform set of standards for the use of exchange rates. Agreements reached by the competent authorities under paragraph 3 need not conform to the internal law provisions of either Contracting State.

Paragraph 4

Paragraph 4 provides that the competent authorities may communicate with each other for the purpose of reaching an agreement. This makes clear that the competent authorities of the two Contracting States may communicate without going through diplomatic channels. Such communication may be in various forms, including, where appropriate, through face-to-face meetings of representatives of the competent authorities.

Paragraph 6 of the 2010 Exchange of Notes

The competent authorities, through consultations, shall develop appropriate bilateral procedures, conditions, methods, and techniques for the implementation of the mutual agreement procedure provided in Article 26. Each competent authority may, in addition, develop unilateral procedures to facilitate the bilateral implementation of the mutual agreement procedure. For guidance in developing such bilateral implementation, the competent authorities will refer to the Best Practices identified in the OECD Manual on Effective Mutual Agreement Procedures.

Treaty termination in relation to competent authority dispute resolution

A case may be raised by a taxpayer after the Convention has been terminated with respect to a year for which a treaty was in force. In such a case the ability of the competent authorities to act is limited. They may not exchange confidential information, nor may they reach a solution that varies from that specified in its law.

Triangular competent authority solutions

International tax cases may involve more than two taxing jurisdictions (e.g., transactions among a parent corporation resident in country A and its subsidiaries resident in countries B and C). As long as there is a complete network of treaties among the three countries, it should be possible, under the full combination of bilateral authorities, for the competent authorities of the three States to work together on a three-sided solution. Although country A may not be able to give information received under Article 27 (Exchange of Information) from country B to the authorities of country C, if the competent authorities of the three countries are working together, it should not be a problem for them to arrange for the authorities of country B to give the necessary information directly to the tax authorities of country C, as well as to those of country A. Each bilateral part of the trilateral solution must, of course, not exceed the scope of the authority of the competent authorities under the relevant bilateral treaty.

Relationship to Other Articles

This Article is not subject to the saving clause of paragraph 4 of the Protocol by virtue of the exception in subparagraph 4(a) of the Protocol. Thus, rules, definitions, procedures, etc., that are agreed upon by the competent authorities under this Article may be applied by the United States with respect to its citizens and residents even if they differ from the comparable Code provisions. Similarly, as indicated above, U.S. law may be overridden to provide refunds of tax to a U.S. citizen or resident under this Article. A person may seek relief under Article 26 regardless of whether he is generally entitled to benefits under Article 24 (Limitation on Benefits). As in all other cases, the competent authority is vested with the discretion to decide whether the claim for relief is justified.

ARTICLE 27 (EXCHANGE OF INFORMATION)

This Article provides for the exchange of information between the competent authorities of the Contracting States.

Paragraph 1

The obligation to obtain and provide information to the other Contracting State is set out in paragraph 1. The information to be exchanged is that which is foreseeably relevant for carrying out the provisions of the Convention or the domestic laws of the United States or Chile concerning taxes of every kind applied at the national level. This language is consistent with the standard of the U.S. and OECD Models. The parties intend for the phrase "is foreseeably relevant" to be interpreted to permit the exchange of information that "may be relevant" for purposes of Code section 7602, which authorizes the IRS to examine "any books, papers, records, or other data which *may be* relevant or material" (emphasis added). In United States v. Arthur Young & Co., 465 U.S. 805, 814 (1984), the Supreme Court stated that the language "may be" reflects Congress's express intention to allow the IRS to obtain "items of even *potential* relevance to an ongoing investigation, without reference to its admissibility." However, the language "may be" would not support a request in which a Contracting State simply asked for information regarding all bank accounts maintained by residents of that Contracting State in the other Contracting State. Thus, the language of paragraph 1 is intended to provide for the exchange of information in tax matters to the widest extent possible, while clarifying that Contracting States are not at liberty to engage in "fishing expeditions" or otherwise to request information that is unlikely to be relevant to the tax affairs of a given taxpayer.

Exchange of information with respect to each State's domestic law is authorized to the extent that taxation under domestic law is not contrary to the Convention. Thus, for example, information may be exchanged with respect to a covered tax, even if the transaction to which the information relates is a purely domestic transaction in the requesting State and, therefore, the exchange is not made to carry out the Convention. An example of such a case is provided in paragraph 8(b) of the OECD Commentary: a company resident in one Contracting State and a company resident in the other Contracting State transact business between themselves through a third-country resident company. Neither Contracting State has a treaty with the third State. To enforce their internal laws with respect to transactions of their residents with the third-country company (since there is no relevant treaty in force), the Contracting States may exchange information regarding the prices that their residents paid in their transactions with the third-country resident.

Paragraph 1 clarifies that information may be exchanged that relates to the assessment or collection of, the enforcement or prosecution in respect of, or the determination of appeals in relation to the taxes covered by the Convention. Thus, the competent authorities may request and provide information for cases under examination or criminal investigation, in collection, on appeals, or under prosecution.

The taxes covered by the Convention for purposes of this Article constitute a broader category of taxes than those referred to in Article 2 (Taxes Covered). Exchange of information is authorized with respect to taxes of every kind imposed by a Contracting State at the national level. Accordingly, information may be exchanged with respect to U.S. estate and gift taxes and excise taxes.

Information exchange is not restricted by paragraph 1 of Article 1 (General Scope). Accordingly, information may be requested and provided under Article 27 with respect to persons who are not residents of either Contracting State. For example, if a third-country resident has a permanent establishment in Chile, and that permanent establishment engages in transactions with a U.S. enterprise, the United States could request information with respect to that permanent establishment, even though the third-country resident is not a resident of either Contracting State. Similarly, if a third-country resident maintains a bank account in Chile, and the Internal Revenue Service has reason to believe that funds in that account should have been reported for U.S. tax purposes but have not been so reported, information can be requested from Chile with respect to that person's account, even though that person is not the taxpayer under examination.

Although the term "United States" does not encompass U.S. possessions for most purposes of the Convention, Code section 7651 authorizes the Internal Revenue Service to utilize the provisions of the Code to obtain information from the U.S. possessions pursuant to a proper request made under Article 27. If necessary to obtain requested information, the Internal Revenue Service could issue and enforce an administrative summons to the taxpayer, a tax authority (or a government agency in a U.S. possession), or a third party located in a U.S. possession.

Paragraph 2

Paragraph 2 provides assurances that any information exchanged will be treated as secret, subject to the same disclosure constraints as information obtained under the laws of the requesting State. Information received may be disclosed only to persons or authorities, including courts and administrative bodies, involved in the assessment, collection, or administration of, the enforcement or prosecution in respect of, or the determination of the of appeals in relation to, the taxes covered by the Convention. The information must be used by these persons in connection with the specified functions. Information may also be disclosed to legislative bodies, such as the tax-writing committees of Congress and the Government Accountability Office, engaged in the oversight of the preceding activities. Information received by these bodies must be for use in the performance of their role in overseeing the administration of U.S. tax laws. Information received may be disclosed in public court proceedings or in judicial decisions.

Paragraph 3

Paragraph 3 provides that the obligations undertaken in paragraphs 1 and 2 to exchange information do not require a Contracting State to carry out administrative measures that are at variance with the laws or administrative practice of either State. Nor is a Contracting State required to supply information not obtainable under the laws or administrative practice of either State, or to disclose trade secrets or other information, the disclosure of which would be contrary to public policy.

Thus, a requesting State may be denied information from the other State if the information would be obtained pursuant to procedures or measures that are broader than those available in the requesting State. However, the statute of limitations of the Contracting State making the request for information should govern a request for information. Thus, the Contracting State of which the request is made should attempt to obtain the information even if its own statute of limitations has passed. In many cases, relevant information will still exist in the business records of the taxpayer or a third party, even though it is no longer required to be kept for domestic tax purposes.

While paragraph 3 states conditions under which a Contracting State is not obligated to comply with a request from the other Contracting State for information, the requested State is not precluded from providing such information, and may, at its discretion, do so subject to the limitations of its domestic law.

Paragraph 4

Paragraph 4 provides that when information is requested by a Contracting State in accordance with this Article, the other Contracting State is obligated to obtain the requested information as if the tax in question were the tax of the requested State, even if that State has no direct tax interest in the case to which the request relates. In the absence of such a paragraph, some taxpayers have argued that subparagraph 3(a) prevents a Contracting State from requesting information from a bank or fiduciary that the Contracting State does not need for its own tax purposes. This paragraph clarifies that paragraph 3 does not impose such a restriction and that a Contracting State is not limited to providing only the information that it already has in its own files.

Paragraph 5

Paragraph 5 provides that a Contracting State may not decline to provide information because that information is held by a bank, other financial institution, nominee or person acting in an agency or fiduciary capacity or because it related to ownership interests in a person. Thus, paragraph 5 would effectively prevent a Contracting State from relying on paragraph 3 to argue that its domestic bank secrecy laws (or similar legislation relating to the disclosure of financial information by financial institutions or intermediaries) override its obligation to provide information under paragraph 1. This paragraph also requires the disclosure of information regarding the beneficial owner of an interest in a person, such as the identity of a beneficial owner of bearer shares.

Paragraph 6

Paragraph 6 provides that the requesting State may specify the form in which information is to be provided (*e.g.*, depositions of witnesses and authenticated copies of unedited original documents). The intention is to ensure that the information may be introduced as evidence in the judicial proceedings of the requesting State. The requested State shall provide the information in the form requested to the same extent that it can obtain information in that form under its own laws and administrative practices with respect to its own taxes.

Paragraph 7

Paragraph 7 states that the competent authorities of the Contracting States will consult with each other for the purpose of cooperating and advising in respect of any action to be taken in implementing this Article. For example, the competent authorities may develop an agreement upon the mode of application of the Article, and may also agree on specific procedures and timetables for the exchange of information. In particular, the competent authorities may agree on minimum thresholds regarding tax at stake or take other measures aimed at ensuring some measure of reciprocity with respect to the overall exchange of information between the Contracting States.

Paragraph 7 of the 2010 Exchange of Notes

With regard to on-site interviews and examinations of books and records, paragraph 7 of the 2010 Exchange of Notes provides that the applicant State will notify the requested State when the applicant State has obtained the consent of persons to be interviewed by officials of the applicant State or for such officials to examine books and records in the possession or control of such consenting persons. Following such interview or examination of books and records, the applicant State may request information or documents related to such interview or examination under Article 27.

Treaty effective dates and termination in relation to exchange of information

Under paragraph 3 of Article 29 (Entry into Force), Article 27 will be effective from the date of entry into force, and, the competent authority may seek information under the Convention without regard to the taxable period to which the matter relates, *i.e.*, such period may be prior to the date of entry into force of the Convention. However, paragraph 20 of the Protocol, as amended by the 2012 Exchange of Notes, provides that, notwithstanding paragraph 3 of Article 29, information covered by paragraph 5 of Article 27, to the extent such information is covered by Article 1 of DFL No. 707 and Article 154 of DFL No. 3 of Chile, shall be available only with respect to bank account transactions that take place on or after January 1, 2010. Other bank information such as signature cards and other account opening documents may be exchanged without regard to the time they were created.

A tax administration may also seek information with respect to a year for which the Convention was in force after the Convention has been terminated. In such a case, the ability of the other tax administration to act is limited. The Convention no longer provides authority for the tax administrations to exchange confidential information. They may only exchange information pursuant to domestic law or other international agreement or arrangement.

ARTICLE 28 (MEMBERS OF DIPLOMATIC MISSIONS AND CONSULAR POSTS)

This Article confirms that any fiscal privileges to which diplomatic or consular officials are entitled under general provisions of international law or under special agreements will apply notwithstanding any provisions to the contrary in the Convention. The agreements referred to include any bilateral agreements, such as consular conventions, that affect the taxation of diplomats and consular officials and any multilateral agreements dealing with these issues, such as the Vienna Convention on Diplomatic Relations and the Vienna Convention on Consular Relations. The United States generally adheres to the latter because its terms are consistent with customary international law.

The Article does not independently provide any benefits to diplomatic agents and consular officers. Article 19 (Government Service) does so, as do Code section 893 and a number of bilateral and multilateral agreements. In the event that there is a conflict between the Convention and international law or such other treaties, under which the diplomatic agent or consular official is entitled to greater benefits under the latter, the latter laws or agreements shall have precedence. Conversely, if the Convention confers a greater benefit than another agreement, the affected person could claim the benefit of the tax treaty.

Pursuant to subparagraph 4(b) of the Protocol, the saving clause of paragraph 4 of the Protocol does not apply to override any benefits of this Article available to an individual who neither is a U.S. citizen nor has been admitted for permanent residence in the United States.

ARTICLE 29 (ENTRY INTO FORCE)

This Article contains the rules for bringing the Convention into force and giving effect to its provisions.

Paragraph 1

Paragraph 1 provides for the ratification of the Convention by both Contracting States according to their constitutional and statutory requirements. The Contracting States will notify each other in writing, through diplomatic channels, when their respective applicable procedures have been satisfied.

In the United States, the process leading to ratification and entry into force is as follows: Once a treaty has been signed by authorized representatives of the two Contracting States, the Department of State sends the treaty to the President who formally transmits it to the Senate for its advice and consent to ratification, which requires approval by two-thirds of the Senators present and voting. Prior to this vote, however, it generally has been the practice for the Senate Committee on Foreign Relations to hold hearings on the treaty and make a recommendation regarding its approval to the full Senate. Both Government and private sector witnesses may testify at these hearings. After the Senate gives its advice and consent to ratification of the treaty, an instrument of ratification is drafted for the President's signature. The President's signature completes the process in the United States.

Paragraph 2

The first sentence of paragraph 2 provides that the Convention will enter into force on the date of the later of the notifications referred to in paragraph 1. The relevant date is the date on the second of these notification documents, and not the date on which the second notification is provided to the other Contracting State.

The date on which a treaty enters into force is not necessarily the date on which its provisions take effect. Paragraph 2, therefore, also contains rules that determine when the provisions of the treaty will have effect.

Under subparagraph 2(a), the Convention will have effect with respect to taxes withheld at source, for amounts paid or credited on or after the first day of the second month following the date on which the Convention enters into force. For example, if the date of the second of the notification documents referred to in paragraph 1 is April 25 of a given year, the withholding rates specified in paragraph 2 of Article 10 (Dividends) would be applicable to any dividends paid or credited on or after June 1 of that year. This rule allows the benefits of the withholding reductions to be put into effect as soon as possible, without waiting until the following year. The delay of one to two months is required to allow sufficient time for withholding agents to be informed about the change in withholding rates. If for some reason a withholding agent withholds at a higher rate than that provided by the Convention (perhaps because it was not able to re-program its computers before the payment is made), a beneficial owner of the income that is a resident of the other Contracting State may make a claim for refund pursuant to Code section 1464.

For all other taxes, subparagraph 2(b) specifies that the Convention will have effect for any taxable period beginning on or after January 1 of the calendar year immediately following the date on which the Convention enters into force.

Paragraph 3

As discussed under Article 27 (Exchange of Information), the powers afforded the competent authority under that Article apply from the date of entry into force of the Convention, regardless of the taxable period to which the matter relates. Paragraph 20 of the Protocol, as amended by the 2012 Exchange of Notes, provides that notwithstanding paragraph 3 of Article 29, information covered by paragraph 5 of Article 27, to the extent that such information is covered by Article 1 of DFL No. 707 and Article 154 of DFL No. 3 of Chile, shall be available only with respect to bank account transactions that take place on or after January 1, 2010. Other bank information such as signature cards and other account opening documents may be exchanged without regard to the time they were created.

ARTICLE 30 (TERMINATION)

Paragraph 1 provides that the Convention is to remain in effect indefinitely, unless terminated by one of the Contracting States in accordance with the provisions of Article 30. Either State may terminate the Convention by giving to the other State a notice of termination in writing through diplomatic channels on or before the thirtieth day of June in any calendar year beginning after the year in which the Convention enters into force. Under subparagraph 2(a), if notice of termination is so given, the provisions of the Convention with respect to taxes withheld at source will cease to have effect for amounts paid or credited on or after January 1 of the calendar year immediately following the date on which such notice is given. Under subparagraph 2(b), with respect to other taxes, the Convention will cease to have effect for taxable periods beginning on or after January 1 of the calendar year immediately following the date on which such notice is given. Under subparagraph 2(c), with respect to provisions of the Convention not covered by subparagraph 2(a) or 2(b), the Convention will cease to have effect on January 1 of the calendar year immediately following the date on which the notice is given.

Article 30 relates only to unilateral termination of the Convention by a Contracting State. Nothing in that Article should be construed as preventing the Contracting States from concluding a new bilateral agreement, subject to ratification, that supersedes, amends or terminates provisions of the Convention without the six-month notification period.

Customary international law observed by the United States and other countries, as reflected in the Vienna Convention on Treaties, allows termination by one Contracting State at any time in the event of a "material breach" of the agreement by the other Contracting State.

OTHER

Paragraph 21 of the Protocol

Paragraph 21 of the Protocol provides a rule regarding the taxation by Chile of certain remittances from pooled investment accounts (such as those established under the Foreign Capital Investment Fund Law No. 18.657, as it may be amended from time to time without changing the general principles thereof). Nothing in the Convention shall restrict the imposition by Chile of tax on remittances from such funds if the fund is required to be administered by a resident of Chile, although the imposition of remittance tax is only permitted in respect of investment in assets situated in Chile. The current tax imposed by Chile on remittances from such funds is 10 percent.

Paragraph 22 of the Protocol

Paragraph 22 of the Protocol provides that the United States and Chile will consult together regarding the terms, operation and application of the Convention to ensure that it continues to serve the purposes of avoiding double taxation and preventing fiscal evasion. Either Contracting State may at any time request that such consultations be conducted expeditiously on matters relating to the terms, operation and application of the Convention which it considers require urgent resolution. The first such consultation in any event will take place within five years of the date on which the Convention enters into force. The Protocol also provides that the United States and Chile will conclude further protocols to amend the Convention, if appropriate. In addition, as explained earlier, paragraph 22 of the Protocol provides that if Chile concludes an income tax treaty with another state that imposes a withholding rate limitation on payments of interest or royalties lower than the limits imposed under paragraph 2 of Article 11 (Interest) or paragraph 2 of Article 12 (Royalties) or that contains terms that further limit the right of the source State to tax capital gains under Article 13 (Capital Gains), the United States and Chile will, at the request of the United States, consult to reassess the balance of benefits of the Convention with a view to concluding a protocol to incorporate such lower rates or limiting terms into the Convention.

www.ingramcontent.com/pod-product-compliance
Lightning Source LLC
Chambersburg PA
CBHW052003280526
45793CB00005B/831